Happy Birthday. 1978

We won't miss

niebuhr so much

with you in the

family! Our love,

Katy & Gorge

REINHOLD NIEBUHR

Makers of the Modern Theological Mind

Bob E. Patterson, Editor

KARL BARTH by *David L. Mueller*
DIETRICH BONHOEFFER by *Dallas M. Roark*
RUDOLF BULTMANN by *Morris Ashcraft*
CHARLES HARTSHORNE by *Alan Gragg*
WOLFHART PANNENBERG by *Don Olive*
TEILHARD DE CHARDIN by *Doran McCarty*
EMIL BRUNNER by *J. Edward Humphrey*
MARTIN BUBER by *Stephen M. Panko*
SOREN KIERKEGAARD by *Elmer H. Duncan*
REINHOLD NIEBUHR by *Bob E. Patterson*
PAUL TILLICH by *John Newport*
GERHARD VON RAD by *James Crenshaw*
HANS KUNG by *John Kiwiet*
ANDERS NYGREN by *Thor Hall*
FRIEDRICH SCHLEIERMACHER by *C. W. Christian*
RICHARD NIEBUHR by *Lonnie Kliever*

Makers of the Modern Theological Mind

Bob E. Patterson, Editor

REINHOLD NIEBUHR

by Bob E. Patterson

Word Books, Publisher, Waco, Texas

REINHOLD NIEBUHR

ISBN 0–87680–508–X
Library of Congress catalog card number: 76–46783
Printed in the United States of America

For Barbara

choice companion
lovely person
and fellow pilgrim

Contents

EDITOR'S PREFACE   9
PREFACE 11
   I. THE MAKING OF A CHRISTIAN REALIST . . . 13
      Niebuhr's Legacy • 13
      The Formative Years • 20
      At the Summit • 39
      The Later Years • 52
  II. EXISTENTIAL ANTHROPOLOGY 63
      The Problem of Man • 64
      The Loss of the Self in Idealism, Naturalism,
         and Romanticism • 67
      Resources from the Christian Faith • 73
 III. MAN THE SINNER 81
      The Origin of Sin • 83
      The Forms of Sin • 87
      Original Sin and Man's Responsibility • 93
      Original Righteousness • 98
 IV. THE TRIUMPH OF GRACE 101
      The Importance of Christ • 103
      Grace as Truth • 105
      Grace as Power • 112

The Paradox of Grace • 116
Eschatological Grace • 121
V. *LOVE AND JUSTICE* 126
The Agape of the Cross • 128
The Relation of Love and Justice • 130
Justice and the Paradox of Grace • 135
Love, Justice, and the Community of Grace • 139
VI. *RELEVANCE AND THE MARCH OF TIME* ... 145
NOTES 155
SELECTED BIBLIOGRAPHY 161

Editor's Preface

Who are the thinkers that have shaped Christian theology in our time? This series tries to answer that question by providing a reliable guide to the ideas of the men who have significantly charted the theological seas of our century. In the current revival of theology, these books will give a new generation the opportunity to be exposed to significant minds. They are not meant, however, to be a substitute for a careful study of the original works of these makers of the modern theological mind.

This series is not for the lazy. Each major theologian is examined carefully and critically—his life, his theological method, his most germinal ideas, his weaknesses as a thinker, his place in the theological spectrum, and his chief contribution to the climate of theology today. The books are written with the assumption that laymen will read them and enter into the theological dialogue that is so necessary to the church as a whole. At the same time they are carefully enough designed to give assurance to a Ph.D. student in theology preparing for his preliminary exams.

Each author in the series is a professional scholar and

theologian in his own right. All are specialists on, and in some cases have studied with, the theologians about whom they write. Welcome to the series.

BOB E. PATTERSON, Editor
Baylor University

Preface

Writing this book has been a labor of gratitude. I first became acquainted with Reinhold Niebuhr's writings when I was a college student. I was at the threshold of my own religious and intellectual pilgrimage, largely untutored and eminently sophomoric. In casting about for something serious in theology to read, I "by chance" picked up Niebuhr's *The Nature and Destiny of Man* in the University library. It was a flawed work, but I could not have deliberately landed on another book written in the last half century by an American author that deserved to be read with more care. It was a muscle-straining experience for me, and because of that initial encounter with Niebuhr I have never again been the same. As the editor of this series of books on "Makers of the Modern Theological Mind," I exercised my privilege of "divine right monarchy" and greedily chose to write on Reinhold Niebuhr myself. More than any other single thinker, Niebuhr deserves credit for helping me see the moral significance of the use of power.

In writing this book I am indebted to others. My thanks go to my secretary, Sharon Massengale, for her skill at the typewriter, and to my graduate assistant, Cecil Taylor, for his skill in research. Both are models of diligence and tolerance. I am grateful to my own Department of Religion for giving me a reduced teaching load to complete this project. I am greatly indebted to Southern Baptist Theological Seminary for allowing me to quote directly and extensively from my doctoral dissertation on Niebuhr written at that institution. Chapters 2–5 in this book reflect the research that I originally did in the dissertation at Southern, and the permission to quote reflects that school's gentle love for its graduates. My sympathy and apology go to my teaching colleagues who have had to put up with my barrage of "Niebuhrisms" at the midmorning faculty coffee break for the last several months. My thanks go to my wife, Barb, who tolerates my Niebuhrian "sin of pride" with good humor, and who encourages me in all my publishing projects. Finally, I am pleased that the people at Word are publishing this series of books on Christian thinkers, that they are my personal friends, and that they are the kind of people who make me glad that I am living in this portion of the twentieth century with them.

I. The Making of a
Christian Realist

NIEBUHR'S LEGACY

When seventy-eight-year-old Reinhold Niebuhr died in
June 1971, America lost its greatest native-born Protestant
theologian since Jonathan Edwards. Niebuhr died serenely
at his home in Stockbridge, Massachusetts—the same town
where Edwards was once banished for his too-demanding
theology—and his funeral was held in the church where
Edwards had preached.

Reinhold Niebuhr's output both as thinker and as activist
was prodigious. His career was long and varied. He was a
parish minister for thirteen years in Detroit; he taught for a
third of a century at Union Theological Seminary in New
York; he was a constant "circuit rider" preacher to colleges
and universities; he was kept busy most of his life with
political activities; he made himself available to all kinds of
people; and he was a prolific writer. He contributed significantly to the fields of theology, philosophy, and the social
sciences. Very few parallel personalities have both interpreted and influenced so many areas of thought. Only age
and illness slowed down his productivity. He was one of the
splendid incredibilities of our time.

He is still too much a part of the contemporary scene for

us to give a final assessment of his major contribution to American life, and it is difficult to know which facet of Niebuhr's many-sidedness to stress. But one thing is certain: Reinhold Niebuhr was the most influential American theologian of this century, the one American who finds a comfortable place in a modern theological pantheon comprised mainly of Europeans. Nearly fifty years ago he instigated an intellectual revolution that changed the climate of theology, and he did more than any other American to shape theology in this country. As the prime theological mover of the last generation, he is holding up remarkably well in this generation. In the present theological confusion he provides solid standing ground. So vibrant was his thought that he provides us a significant instance in which dialogue "with a thinker of the past" can be most profitable. His successors cannot avoid dealing with his forceful insights; they will have to abandon them deliberately or build on them. He remains a helpful guide in interpreting the agonies of the twentieth century American religious and political life. His spirited polemics are still worthy targets against which young theologians should test their skills.

Niebuhr claimed that he was not a theologian; and he was not, in the sense of having worked out an elaborate system such as that of the German theologian Karl Barth or the émigré to America Paul Tillich. He felt that only those who had developed a full philosophical-religious system of their own were entitled to the designation "theologian." "Bastardized theology" was the way he spoke self-mockingly of his attempts, but this was because he was modest about his scholarship. Niebuhr was so incredibly busy it is hard to imagine him sitting quietly in his study long enough to write a *Church Dogmatics.* Niebuhr said, "I cannot and do not claim to be a theologian. . . . I have never been very competent in the nice points of pure theology; and I must confess that I have not been sufficiently interested heretofore to acquire the competence." [1] Niebuhr said that he had been frequently challenged to prove that his interests were theological rather than practical, but, he said, "I have always refused to enter a defense, partly because I thought the point was well taken and partly because the distinction did not interest me." [2] In truth, he added little to the theological quest for a more precise understanding of God and Christ. Even in the area of his greatest contribution, the doctrine of man, he was too polemical to be confined to the formal structures of theology. Yet he is still best categorized as a theologian, and both his activity and thought give the "academic" theologians something to write about. As one of the greatest theological minds of the twentieth century and the foremost interpreter of American religious social behavior, he restated for America the great themes of Christian theology in a revolutionary way. The fact that he was a preacher, teacher, politician, and journalist may obscure his major role as theologian. No apology is made for including him in the "Makers of the Modern Theological Mind" series, since he did some of the most vigorous theological thinking of the twentieth century.

The central focus of Niebuhr's career was "the defense and justification of the Christian faith in a secular age, particularly among what Schleiermacher called Christianity's 'intellectual despisers.'" [3] He felt that Christianity gained self-knowledge as it grappled with its secular competitors. But Niebuhr did not defend or justify the Christian faith in the traditional manner, since he felt that the "Christian apologists cannot hope for too much success." [4] His apologetic was a twofold polemic, on the one hand against the secular and pagan world and on the other hand against the household of faith, the church. His stance against both was stringently iconoclastic: he brought judgment upon falsehood in both secular and ecclesiastical camps.

He launched his attack against both church and world from a base of prophetic biblical theology—"biblical realism," as he called it. Rather than accommodating Christianity to what is already proximately Christian in our culture, he assumed all along that the insights of biblical faith are more true and profound than any secular alternatives. He sought to disarm the secularist by proving that alternative faiths to Christianity are inadequate while showing the cogency and relevance of Christianity. He was just as vigorous in criticizing the church's tendency either to bless some particular social or economic order as the only Christian one, or completely to ignore secular culture. For example, both secular and religious idealism (messianic Marxism and the Protestant social gospel movement) assumed that society would automatically improve through moral and pious benevolence. On the contrary, Niebuhr argued, the collective egoism of class, race, and nation is more persistent than the self-regard of the individual. Man is neither perfectible, as idealists in religion and philosophy had supposed, nor the controllable object of nature, as described by materialists.

Both secular and religious optimism led to moral and political confusion because they ignored man's sin of willful pride—a universally entrenched, predatory self-interest that exists in all men. Protestant liberalism formally acknowledged the concept of individual sin but widely ignored the idea as a potentially meaningful element in normal life. Utopian Marxism recognized evil but located it outside of man in property. Only the biblical idea of original sin, Niebuhr maintained, properly underlines man's potential for both good and evil, for realizing perfection and for spoiling it. Niebuhr, taking the doctrine of original sin seriously but not literally, believed that the biblical image of man conveyed a deeper understanding of the human situation than any alternate scheme. He felt that the biblical portrayal of the human predicament could liberate the liberal mind from its rationalistic fixations, show the limitations of all human schemes, and save men from guilty despair when their visions did not bring in the Kingdom of God. In some twenty books and a thousand articles he restored words like *sin, grace, judgment, conscience, obligation,* and *mercy* to the American vocabulary, showing believers and skeptics alike that the Christian message can deal realistically with the modern world. His penchant for polemic against both secularist and saint made his theology dialectical rather than systematic.

Niebuhr's theology always sought practical expression, and social ethics was the route this expression took. He tried to reconcile an "apparently" mutually exclusive absolute Christian ethic (agape) with a relative social ethic (justice). In combining theology and social ethics he brought theological ethics into the social arena. This thrust him into political involvements in a manner almost unique in his profession. His political biography shows the nature of his alignments: social disillusionment with both capitalism and Marxism; embracement of pacifism, and then the abandonment of it during the rise of American isolationism and European fascism in the 1930s; the championing of U.S. intervention in World War II and a cold war stratagem to contain Soviet power; and indictment of the pretensions of American messianism and scientism when the U.S. first intervened militarily in Viet Nam under John F. Kennedy. In the process of giving theology a practical expression he shaped a distinctively American social ethic that dominated Protestant thought in America from the close of World War I to the widening of the war in Viet Nam. Political ethics as a central theological discipline now has a new intellectual identity and dignity, and many of today's young "political theologians" owe their ancestry to his creative work.

Niebuhr's prophetic politics, steeped in biblical theology, Greek classics, Western history and philosophy, depth psychology, and shrewd economic analysis, was the intellectual salvation of some of the most secular of statesmen and scholars. No American preacher or teacher has made a greater contribution to secular political wisdom and moral responsibility. George F. Kennan called him "the father of us all," and Hans J. Morgenthau said that he was perhaps the only creative American political philosopher since Calhoun. Both Kennan and Morgenthau interpreted errors in American foreign policy with insights specifically derived from Niebuhr. William Pfaff and Edmund Stillman have benefited from Niebuhr's showing how America has been deceived by its own pride in misunderstanding its role in history. He has influenced the pragmatic liberalism of many prominent Americans, some of whom saw him as a practical strategist and theoretical interpreter of politics (Walter Lippmann, George Kennan, James Reston, and Hans Morgenthau) while others are convinced that he was chiefly a philosopher of history (Arthur Schlesinger, Jr., Will Herberg, and Charles Frankel). Niebuhr's comments on U.S. domestic and foreign policy, particularly after World War II, powerfully influenced some of the ablest people in public life. Some sentences in *The Arrogance of Power*, former Senator William F. Fulbright's work, are nearly interchangeable with sentences in *The Nature and Destiny of Man*. Martin Luther King, Jr., in a BBC interview shortly before his death, acknowledged Niebuhr as one of the two major intellectual influences in his life. Even when these prominent policymakers have ignored the Christian theology behind Niebuhr's realistic awareness, they have approached their history and experience with new and significant insights.

Niebuhr's way with words was evident in both his teaching and preaching. He was a most quotable theologian. Some of his balanced epigrams have become classics. His literary output was enormous, and, according to biographer June Bingham, if "you go to look him up in any library file, you might as well take along a picnic lunch." [5] Among his students at Union Seminary he was a much-loved lecturer and conversationalist. He kept his students breathless with fast-paced, challenging lectures. He enjoyed arguments over lunch in the seminary cafeteria, sometimes roughly caricaturing his opponents, and these dialogues often ran over into late evening sessions in his own apartment. He was one of the great Christian preachers of this century, and it is a pity that he allowed only two volumes of his sermons to be printed. For years he was a "circuit rider" pulpiteer to colleges and universities, devoting his weekends to explaining the basics of Christianity to students who knew little, and often cared less, about them. He was immensely popular in many of the great churches of the country. "Those who faced his lucid and mercurial brilliance from the pew will surely agree that their deepest impression has been that of an enormously shrewd and worldly intelligence whose overriding interest centers in the special kind of illumination that is cast by the Christian faith upon the major perplexities of modern man," says Nathan A. Scott, Jr.[6]

Niebuhr influenced the literary community, but here his influence is more difficult to measure than in the areas of theology, political thought, social action, or the pulpit and classroom. His influence was felt in both contemporary criticism and creative literature, but his presence was there more often "in the nuances of stress and intonation than in the form of documented reference."[7] Scott, a careful Niebuhr-watcher, who cataloged Niebuhr's influence on the literary world, has said that Niebuhr made some writers aware of the tragic character of all human action. F. O. Matthiessen, for example, acknowledged Niebuhr's influence on his critique of the nineteenth-century belief in every man as his own messiah in *American Renaissance*. Scott has also said that Niebuhr's influence can probably be traced in the critical assessment of various forms of liberalism by Lionel Trilling, Robert Penn Warren (*Brother to Dragons*), and Frederick Buechner (*The Return of Ansel Gibbs*).

Niebuhr influenced countless lives both directly and indirectly. A charming story about his impact concerns the so-called Serenity Prayer in constant use by the half-million acknowledged alcoholics in Alcoholics Anonymous groups throughout the world: "O God, give us serenity to accept what cannot be changed, courage to change what should be changed, and wisdom to distinguish the one from the other."

In 1934 Niebuhr preached at a small church near his sum-
mer home in Heath, Massachusetts, and he had casually
jotted down the prayer on a slip of paper to use in the worship. At the conclusion of the service, his next-door neighbor
Howard Chandler Robbins, dean of the Cathedral of St. John
the Divine, requested a copy of the prayer. Handing him the
slip of paper, Niebuhr said, "Here, take the prayer. I have
no further use for it." Robbins included the prayer in a sub-
sequent issue of the Cathedral *News*, whence it gradually
made its way into the religious public domain of America.

THE FORMATIVE YEARS

Reinhold Niebuhr was born in Wright City, Missouri, on
June 21, 1892, and his boyhood was spent in St. Charles,
Missouri, and Lincoln, Illinois. His father was a German
immigrant who served as pastor in a German-speaking
Lutheran Church which mixed the Lutheran and Reformed
traditions. Niebuhr said that the "first formative religious
influence on my life was my father." [8] He was nurtured on
German-Lutheran piety in his father's parishes in Missouri
and Illinois. At ten he told his father he had decided to become a minister because "you are the most interesting man
in town." He studied at two Lutheran schools, Elmhurst College and Eden Theological Seminary. Elmhurst was a small,
then-unaccredited school run by his denomination, the Evangelical Synod of North America, now part of the United
Church of Christ. In April 1913, while Reinhold was still at
Eden, his father suffered an attack of diabetes, went into a
coma, and died.

Eager to break away from his tightly knit German church
life and encouraged by his mother, he studied for two further
years at the Divinity School of Yale University, concentrating his study in the problems of epistemology and receiving
a Master of Arts degree. He said that he got into Yale only
because they were "hard up for students," but he went on to

earn himself a respected academic place in this Ivy League school.

At Yale he was deeply influenced by liberal social thought and became a typical product of the early twentieth-century liberal theology. As a student he shared the liberal temper of the campus. He accepted the historical-critical method of biblical studies, rejected some traditional theological claims on the basis of their incredibility to a critical mind, assumed a religious optimism, championed individualism, accepted evolutionary categories, emphasized ethics, stressed the humanity of Jesus, and recognized the importance of toleration. At this point he discontinued his formal education because of family needs and because studies "bored me . . . and frankly the other side of me came out; I desired relevance rather than scholarship." [9] Long before it became academically popular to wed thought with action, Niebuhr was developing a life-style in which his theology was hammered out in the context of pressing human needs. This in part explains why his thought altered significantly through more than half a century.

Rather than stay at Yale and work toward his doctorate, Niebuhr accepted the appointment by his denomination as pastor of Bethel Evangelical Church in Detroit, Michigan, in 1915. Family needs "and my boredom with epistemology prompted me to forswear graduate study and the academic career to which it pointed," he said.[10] (Although he never earned a Ph.D. degree, he was awarded eighteen honorary doctorates, including one from Oxford.) His widowed mother moved to Detroit with him and managed the affairs of the parsonage, living with him until his marriage in 1931.

This little congregation was composed of eighteen families, but in the next thirteen years under Niebuhr's leadership its membership was to reach nearly eight hundred. During these years Detroit's population grew threefold, from half a million to a million and a half, and became the motor capital of the country as the automobile industry rapidly expanded.

These two facts "determined my development more than any
books which I may have read," Niebuhr commented.[11] Niebuhr called Detroit a "frontier" industrial town, but his diary
indicates he was obviously happy in his pastorate. (Pages
from his 1915–1928 diary were edited and published in 1929
with the title *Leaves from the Notebook of a Tamed Cynic*.)

Youthful high spirits, unfortunately, do not automatically
solve pastoral problems. His mother became, in effect, the
assistant pastor to the fledgling twenty-three-year-old minister, and he was grateful for her help. In his first *Leaves*
entry in 1915 he wrote, "Where did anyone ever learn in a
seminary how to conduct or help with a Ladies Aid meeting?
I am glad that mother has come to live with me and will take
care of that part of the job." [12] But after three months he
admitted that he was discouraged over his preaching: "Now
that I have preached about a dozen sermons I find that I am
repeating myself. A different text simply means a different
pretext for saying the same thing over again." [13] The few
ideas that he had worked into sermons at the seminary were
soon used up, and it was a full five years before he admitted
that he was beginning to "like" the preaching ministry. He
wrote, "I think since I have stopped worrying so much about
the intellectual problems of religion and have begun explor-
ing some of its ethical problems there is more of a thrill in
preaching." [14]

Niebuhr became a successful pastor. Sensitive to the personal problems of his parishioners, he learned many Christian
skills and attitudes at a practical level. Shortly after taking
charge of his parish, he discovered that two elderly ladies
in his congregation who were dying were counting on him to
help them face death peacefully. From one's prayerful and
wholesome acceptance of death he saw how the Christian
faith can work. He said, "I relearned the essentials of the
Christian faith at the bedside of that nice old soul." [15] At the
bedside of the other he saw how faith can be blocked by
those who are pridefully preoccupied with themselves. It was

typical of Niebuhr that this lesson stayed with him. Reflecting in later years on the difference between the faiths of the two old ladies, he said that the "church is a curiously mixed body consisting of those who have never been shaken in their self-esteem or self-righteousness and who use the forms of religion for purposes of self-aggrandizement; and of the true Christians who live by 'a broken spirit and a contrite heart.' " [16]

He could learn from all sorts and conditions of people. Niebuhr drew theological insights from the social gospel (a concern for social justice), from Karl Marx (men are influenced by their place in the social scheme), from Augustine (history is moved by both love and sin), and Kierkegaard (the free individual is anxious), but his first lessons came from personal experience. Niebuhr was reluctant to place himself visibly near the center of his written work, but he did confess that facts, not books, shaped his theology. He said that even at Union Seminary "the gradual unfolding of my theological ideas came not so much through study as through the pressure of world events." [17] Niebuhr's own self-interpretative clue, then, is that he moved from practice to ethics to theological formulation. Martin E. Marty says of Niebuhr that it "is possible to trace almost every eventually developed view of the religious community in action back to his root experience in the Detroit parish." [18]

Even though his church grew rapidly in membership, he was a constant lecturer and preacher on college campuses, a writer for religious and secular journals, a participant in political and secular affairs, and a traveler abroad. In 1924 he chaired the large Detroit meeting for La Follette for President. Entering politics that year at the national level, he never withdrew from involvement. Sherwood Eddy, a leading figure in the YMCA, was so impressed with Niebuhr's speaking ability that he contributed money to hire an assistant at Bethel Church and thus free Niebuhr to be a roving ambassador to college campuses. Niebuhr wrote that for years "I

commuted, as it were, between ecclesiastical and academic
communities. I found each with a sense of superiority over
the other either because it possessed, or had discarded, the
Christian faith." [19] He published his first article in 1916 (in
The Atlantic Monthly), and during the remainder of his
parish ministry published some forty more signed articles
(mostly in *The Christian Century, The World Tomorrow,*
and *The Atlantic*). He was emerging as a writer worth
watching.

His service as pastor of Bethel Church proved to be of
decisive influence in the development of his thought and
interest. Here he discovered industrial America. Here his
moral passion was honed as he observed firsthand the fierce
struggle between management and labor. His own congregation was a cross-section of wage earners and the wealthy.
The problems of social ethics came into focus for him. He
committed himself to the cause of the working class and
began actively to criticize the detrimental consequences of
capitalism. His pastoral rounds brought him into contact
with the victims of the industrial dehumanization. His sermons from his own pulpit made him one of the interesting
men in town, and potentially one of the most dangerous to
Henry Ford I. Niebuhr said, "I cut my eyeteeth fighting
Ford."

Ford, appealing to humanitarian motives to justify his
economic policies, came to represent for Niebuhr the capitalistic system. Supposedly Ford's policies in the automobile
industry were producing great profits for workers, but Niebuhr observed that these policies were reducing workers to
mere cogs in an impersonal assembly line while producing
great profits for Ford himself.

Mother and I visited at the home of ———— today where the husband is sick and was out of employment before he became sick.
The folks have few connections in the city. They belong to no
church. What a miserable existence it is to be friendless in a large
city. And to be dependent on a heartless industry. The man is

about 55 or 57 I should judge, and he is going to have a desperate time securing employment after he gets well.[20]

Niebuhr openly scoffed at Ford's trumpeted magnanimity, and welcomed union rallies in his church when other public platforms closed to them. He placed himself on the side of the underdog and the Bethel Church stood loyally behind him.

In Detroit Niebuhr discovered the real cost of industrialization: dehumanization of the worker, nervous tensions, unemployment without compensation, broken bodies, appalling working conditions in the factories, and naïve gentlemen with a genius for mechanics deciding the lives and fortunes of hundreds of thousands. At this time Niebuhr was driven into the mild socialism of the "Social Gospel," but he soon began to do battle against what he called its naïveté (its lack of understanding of the depths of sin in individual and society). His Detroit experience posed for him the problems with which he would struggle throughout his career—racial strife, economic injustice, international disorder, and an adequate theology. Detroit was to see the beginning of Niebuhr's pragmatism, that ability to break away from the givens that his biographer June Bingham calls "the courage to change." Detroit was the learning laboratory for him as he moved from parish ministry to public protester.

During these years his theology underwent a significant change. He entered his parish with the moralistic assumptions of optimistic liberalism, the goodness of man and the inevitability of human progress, but he soon saw that corrupting self-interest is inextricably involved in the human situation. Looking back upon his ministry in later years, he confessed, "About midway in my ministry, which extends roughly from the peace of Versailles to the peace of Munich, measured in terms of Western history, I underwent a fairly complete conversion of thought which involved rejection of almost all the liberal theological ideals with which I ventured forth in 1915." [21]

Serving as a minister in an auto workers' community, he was shocked by the callous injustice of a modern industrial society. He was equally shocked to find that the Christian church as he knew it was isolated from men's needs by social impotence. This early insight into the ugly realities of an industrial society, particularly the exploitation of men by other men and the church's placid indifference, was to change his pastoral ministry. He said that it began to dawn upon him that "the simple little moral homilies which were preached in that as in other cities, by myself and others, seemed completely irrelevant to the brutal facts of life in a great industrial center. Whether irrelevant or not, they were certainly futile. They did not change human actions or attitudes in any problem of collective behavior by a hair's breadth, though they may well have helped to preserve private amenities and to assuage individual frustrations." [22] He developed a passion for a realistic theology which would be relevant to man's total life in twentieth-century American society. His Detroit experience began to show him that there were two *false* answers to the problem of relating gospel and world. He revolted against a theology to the left ("liberalism") and a theology to the right ("orthodoxy") in seeking an answer to them ("Christian realism").

Niebuhr began his career as a liberal, but he became one of liberalism's most ardent critics. He said, "In my parish duties I found that the simple idealism into which the classical faith had evaporated was as irrelevant to the crises of personal life as it was to the complex social issues of an industrial city." [23] With a predilection for exaggeration, he isolated liberalism's confidence in moral progress and directed his polemics against this feature. The illusion of moral progress became the central theme in his attack. He said, "Modern liberalism is steeped in a religious optimism which is true to the facts of neither the world of nature nor the world of history." [24] World War I shattered for Niebuhr liberalism's optimistic view of life. He felt that nationalism

and liberalism had combined in an unhealthy union of righteousness and power to urge on the war in moral terms.
Liberal churches were prostituted at the hands of nationalism.
After the war he regretted his defense of it, concluding that
the war was a contest of power dependent upon economic
interests. He decided not to have anything to do with "the
war business" again and became a pacifist.

Niebuhr began a heated and ceaseless struggle against
both the ethical inadequacy and the theological presuppositions of liberalism. Liberalism for Niebuhr had two forms,
religious and secular. The religious form was the theology
characterized by the American Social Gospel movement,
initiated by Walter Rauschenbusch at the beginning of this
century and having its roots in the prevailing theology of
Europe in the nineteenth century and in American "revival-
ism." The Social Gospel movement tried to change America's
unjust social systems by convincing the men who controlled
and managed the systems to live by the Sermon on the
Mount. This overweening confidence grew out of a theology
which had a superficial view of man's sinfulness, which identified the Kingdom of God with current political and philosophical ideals, and which pictured man as having a "spark
of the divine" in him and thus capable of his own salvation.

Niebuhr found Protestant liberalism to be incompetent and
irrelevant, to be little more than a system of values descend-
ing from the Enlightenment. It was no better than the piety
of bourgeois idealism with its naïve preachments about moral
optimism, its identification of the ideal society with the
Kingdom of God, and its simple confidence in the possibility
of implementing in public life the absolutes of the Christian
faith. His first book, published in 1927, *Does Civilization
Need Religion?*, was a direct consequence of his Detroit experience and reflected Niebuhr's alarm at the depersonalization
caused by an industrial civilization. He said that his "early
writings were characterized by a critical attitude toward the
'liberal' world view, whether expressed in secular or Christian

terms." [25] Liberal Protestantism was so much at home in the
world that it had no counsel and had become a harmless
adornment of the moral life. The Social Gospel movement
with its happy worldliness had lost its capacity for genuinely
radical criticism. The book represented his break with liberalism, but it did not contain the thorough realism of his later
writings. The book was a prelude to his later attack on
liberalism from a Marxist perspective during the 1930s and
his Augustinian-inspired attack in the 1940s.

The secular form of liberalism for Niebuhr was a philosophy and social ethic which stemmed from a secularized Social Gospel combined with American optimism, faith in the
techniques of natural science, and the idea of inevitable
social progress. Secular liberalism appealed to "reason"
rather than the Sermon on the Mount in order to achieve the
perfect society. According to the tradition of Locke, Jefferson,
Mill, and John Dewey, social injustice grew out of ignorance,
and could be obliterated through education and the power
of moral suasion. Niebuhr became convinced that this mild
Pelagianism did not understand the element of power in the
living actualities of politics and could not be expected to
provide any relevant guidance for social structures.

In Detroit Niebuhr learned that neither form of liberalism
was relevant to the brutal facts of life in an industrial culture
or a collective society. The corrupting elements of self-
interest remain mixed with man's best intentions. The potentiality for progress is always accompanied by the potentiality
for destructiveness. Man is imperfect and history is incomplete. Moving from liberalism's inadequacy, he began to
criticize its theologically weak view of God and man, demanding a more "transcendent" view of God and a more "realistic" view of collective man. While trying to preserve
liberalism's valid insight of man's moral and rational capacity for good, Niebuhr rejected its utopian and individualistic
social strategy. Accepting liberalism's spirit (openness to
change), he turned his back on its creed (the painless im-

provability of man). Through this type of criticism Niebuhr
introduced into American theology the movement known as
Christian realism, and he remained its outstanding leader.

As liberalism was a false answer to social-ethical problems on the left, so "orthodoxy" was a smaller but still
formidable enemy on the right. Orthodoxy was synonymous
in his thought with conventional Christianity (biblical literalism, fundamentalism, Lutheranism, and Calvinism). Niebuhr directed most of his polemic against liberal churches,
possibly because he seemed to have despaired of theological
fundamentalism and felt it was beyond redemption. He saw
in Detroit that orthodoxy was as inadequate as liberalism in
dealing with modern ethical problems. It neglected man's
present concerns by concentrating on his eternal destiny, it
neglected public morals by restricting itself to individual
perfection, and it sanctioned social evil with its doctrine of
predestination.

Niebuhr wrote in his Detroit diary in 1928:

> One of the most fruitful sources of self-deception in the ministry
> is the proclamation of great ideals and principles without any clue
> to their relation to the controversial issues of the day. The minister
> feels very heroic in uttering the ideals because he knows that some
> rather dangerous immediate consequences are involved in their
> application. But he doesn't make the application clear, and those
> who hear his words are either unable to see the immediate issue
> involved or they are unconsciously grateful to the preacher for not
> belaboring a contemporaneous issue which they know to be in-
> volved but would rather not face.[26]

Even though orthodoxy actually contributed to unjust social structures by its neglect, it did contribute to a realistic
social ethic with its doctrine of sin. Niebuhr took the traditional Protestant doctrine of original sin, stripped it of its
literalism, and used it to explain the real character of modern
society. His criticism of biblical literalism drove him back
to an acceptance of "biblical realism" (to use his own
phrase), to the biblical answer to sin, and the biblical affirma-

tion of God's grace in Christ. His emphasis on man's sinfulness soon made Niebuhr a revolutionary force in American
theology. He set himself the task of steering a realistic course
between the two threats of liberalism and orthodoxy as he
tried to relate Christianity to the modern world.

During World War I Niebuhr had traveled to Europe on
speaking tours with the YMCA leader, Sherwood Eddy. Eddy
drew him onto the national stage and gave him a larger
audience by providing speaking opportunities on college
campuses. Niebuhr soon had the opportunity to position himself at the crossroads of American intellectual and political
ferment. At Eddy's instigation, Niebuhr spoke before a student convention in Detroit in 1923. Henry Sloane Coffin
(later president of Union Seminary in New York City), who
was in the audience and became acquainted with Niebuhr, in
time offered Niebuhr a teaching post at Union in the field of
Applied Christianity. When Niebuhr asked, "What shall I
teach?" Coffin replied, "Just what you think." Niebuhr said
this was "a hazardous venture, since my reading in the
parish had been rather undisciplined and I had no scholarly
competence in my field, not to speak of the total field of
Christian theology." [27]

The tall, balding Niebuhr resigned his Detroit pastorate in
1928 and joined the faculty of Union to start full-time teaching. Having learned to love the pastorate, he left his congregation with reluctance. He also was well aware of his lack
of preparation for the classroom. He said, "It was a full
decade before I could stand before a class and answer the
searching questions of the students at the end of a lecture
without the sense of being a fraud who pretended to a larger
and more comprehensive knowledge than I possessed." [28] His
life in New York was even more hectic than it had been in
Detroit as he taught, preached, traveled, wrote, and partici-
pated in a growing number of both religious and secular
organizations. His presence helped make that period the
golden age for Union, and he remained there until his retirement in 1960.

He was too much of a human being to live alone, and three years after he went to Union he married one of his students, a bright, elegant Briton. Ursula Keppel-Compton was an honor student at Oxford before coming to Union in 1930. Mrs. Niebuhr was not only a warm and vivacious companion, but demonstrated her own theological alertness by teaching religion at Barnard College for many years. They had two children, a son and a daughter, Christopher and Elizabeth, who added to their happy home life. Mrs. Niebuhr, a woman of impressive erudition, later became head of the religion department at Barnard College. Included in the Niebuhr teaching dynasty were his late brother, H. Richard, the eminent Yale ethicist; his late sister, Hulda, who taught education at McCormick Seminary; and his nephew, Harvard theologian Richard Reinhold Niebuhr. The two brothers were to dominate the thought of American Christian ethics for four decades.

The academic environment at Union with its research facilities stimulated Niebuhr to publish theological writings that were to have a notable impact both nationally and internationally. He became one of the most prolific writers in American intellectual life. Since it is unlikely that the general reader can take the time and effort to read all of Niebuhr's books (not to mention his hundreds of journal articles), I have tried in this chapter to intersperse mention of his books in the chronology of his life, note their contents, show their place in his developing thought, and point to their impact on American thought. It is my hope that this hasty survey will allow the general reader to turn to several of Niebuhr's most important books without the feeling that he is totally disoriented in the mass and variety of Niebuhr's writings.

Niebuhr's lecturing and writing never removed him from the problems of the day on the one hand nor from the church on the other. If anything, he became more deeply involved in the arena of social action and political debate, but from his basic home in the seminary's Christian community. He never hesitated to join a movement promoting social justice, and during the thirties and forties he lent his name to more than a hundred of them—a matter of some amusement to his friends. Whereas in Detroit he had learned the resources for practical justice in the Hebrew-Christian tradition, in New York he learned of such resources among the secularists as well. A number of radical and liberal groups were surprised to find a minister among their number and in accord with their views. He was a pioneer in the Christian rediscovery of the secular—the healthy affirmation that God's grace (the hidden Christ) is also at work outside the church. In 1929 he served on the executive committee of the League for Independent Political Action and was still active in the Fellowship of Reconciliation, the leading pacifist organization on the American scene. In 1930 he helped found the Fellowship of Socialist Christians and ran for Congress as the candidate of the Socialist party in the Morningside Heights community of New York City. As he moved theologically to the right, he became a well-known figure in the radical political circles of the left. Capable of change, Niebuhr was ever a "moving target" in both body and mind for his critics.

As Niebuhr contemplated the shambles of the Depression, he became deeply convinced that modern liberalism, whether in its secular or its religious form, could not provide relevant guidance for social and political reconstruction. Out of this disenchantment with liberalism came his famous book of 1932, *Moral Man and Immoral Society*. This book, representing Niebuhr's first venture into political philosophy, had an explosive effect in American theological circles. It carried the same impact in America that Barth's commentary on Romans carried in Europe. His academic colleagues at Union were taken aback by his brash, outspoken touting of socialism and pacifism when he joined the faculty, but they were even less ready when he attacked theological and political liberalism in this book. No other book in the first third of the twentieth century had a greater impact in American theological circles. Many old liberals looked upon this book as a study in ruthless iconoclasm, demolishing their dearest assumptions and removing the foundation for a Christian philosophy. Later, Niebuhr was jokingly to say that an even more accurate title for his book would have been "Immoral Man and Even More Immoral Society."

Niebuhr, wrestling with the contrast between individual and group ethics, summarized the problem in the following way:

> A realistic analysis of the problems of human society reveals a constant and seemingly irreconcilable conflict between the needs of society and the imperatives of a sensitive conscience. This conflict, which could be most briefly defined as the conflict between ethics and politics, is made inevitable by the double focus of the moral life. One focus is in the inner life of the individual, and the other in the necessities of man's social life. From the perspective of society the highest moral ideal is justice. From the perspective of the individual the highest ideal is unselfishness. Society must strive for justice, even if it is forced to use means, such as self-assertion, resistance, coercion, and perhaps resentment, which cannot gain the moral sanction of the most sensitive and moral spirit. The individual must strive to realize his life by losing and finding himself in something greater than himself. . . . Political morality, in other words, is in the most uncompromising antithesis to religious morality.[29]

Niebuhr felt that no reconstruction could take place until a sober assessment of power had been given. He asserted that social collectives are so egotistical that a tolerable justice can be achieved only by guaranteeing enough power to each group to counterbalance the power of other groups by which they may be exploited.

Niebuhr said that the thesis of his book was that a "sharp distinction must be drawn between the moral and social behavior of individuals and of social groups, national, racial, and economic; and that this distinction justifies and necessitates political policies which a purely individualistic ethic must always find embarrassing." [30] He said that all moralists misunderstood the brutal character of groups. "Whatever increase in social intelligence and moral good will may be achieved in human history, may serve to mitigate the brutalities of social conflict, but they cannot abolish the conflict itself." [31] As groups increase in size they become more selfish, and perhaps "the most significant moral characteristic of a nation is its hypocrisy." [32] Individual moral life is difficult enough, but a "perennial weakness of the moral life in individuals is simply raised to the nth degree in national life." [33]

Niebuhr said that the relevant norm for political decisions and social policy is not love, as the liberals had claimed, but justice. Whereas it may be possible to bring about just relations between individuals by moral and rational persuasion, in larger groups this is an impossibility. The relations between large groups, therefore, must be predominantly based on power rather than ethics. Power is as significant as moral persuasion in large groups, and a just society is the result of politics rather than education. Any thought to the contrary is pure sentimentality, he argued.

It was this position that led Niebuhr eventually to disavow his mild socialism and to abandon the position of pacifism. To abandon force for moral persuasion is to invite disaster, he felt. The trouble with pacifism, Niebuhr finally came to say, was that it tried to live in history without sinning. Violence was a part of the class struggle, he felt, and conceded the right of violence to the underprivileged classes. At the beginning of World War II he developed the fullest argument in the American church against pacifism. He fully recognized the evil of war, but judged it less evil than acquiescence to Nazi tyranny. He became more vocal in his opposition to appeasement, and backed many causes that aided refugees fleeing Hitler's Europe. Paul Tillich credited Niebuhr with having saved his life at the time Hitler came to power. As Niebuhr took on international prominence as a

molder of opinion he developed working relationships with
people in the left wing Democratic party and the major news
media, notably Eleanor Roosevelt and the Luce publications
Time and *Life*. He began his long association with government policy-makers in the State Department and was gradually drawn into the orbit of American leadership as a
consultant.

Niebuhr published another book in 1932 that went un-
noticed in the shadow of *Moral Man and Immoral Society*.
Two years earlier he had given a series of lectures to social
workers, and these lectures formed the basis of the book
The Contribution of Religion to Social Work. In this book he
argued that religion created a conscience which is quick to
understand social need, that religious philanthropy gives
charitably but without raising ultimate questions about the
causes of social maladjustment, that religion "unifies individuals, stabilizes societies, creates social imagination and
sanifies social life; but it also perpetuates ancient evils, increases social inertia, creates illusions and preserves super-
stitions." [34] He also argued that religion is a resource for the
social worker because it contains potentials for achieving a
more adequate social justice. Because of the brevity of the
book, the special audience to which it was addressed, and the
untimeliness of its publication, it is seldom quoted from or
mentioned by even the most ardent Niebuhr followers.

In 1934 he published *Reflections on the End of an Era,* in
which he continued to argue for a realistic political theory
that would set power against power and bring about a more
just social system. Niebuhr said that the basic conviction running through the book was that "the liberal culture of
modernity is quite unable to give guidance and direction to
a confused generation which faces the disintegration of a
social system and the task of building a new one." [35] In this
book he confidently expected the collapse of capitalism—
words he was later to eat publicly. He made a twofold pro-
posal for spiritual guidance—first, a more radical political

orientation, and second, a more conservative religious conviction (a return to more classical and historical interpretations)—but without hope that either would be heeded. He
admitted that his approach would "satisfy neither the liberals
in politics and religion, nor the political radicals nor the
devotees of traditional Christianity." [36] Niebuhr struggled to
find a new standing place in the Christian camp, struggled to
be heard by the secularist, and feared all the while that he
would be ignored by both church and world.

His continuing reaction against moral liberalism led him
to accept some insights from Marxism. He was never a
Marxist and was ever critical of its reckless fanaticism which
led to inordinate political tyranny. He never had any illusions
about its demonic character and was one of its more severe
critics. However, to criticize liberalism he used Marxism's
organic view of society, its theory of class conflict, its insights into social injustice, its intuition of judgment and
disaster, and its sense for the duplicity of man. He deplored
Marxism's moral cynicism, but praised its realism.

He was to become one of the sharpest critics of the religious pretensions and failures of Marxism. He felt that
Marxism had chosen the wrong means (violence) to bring
about the ideal society, that it destroyed the good along
with the bad in its revolution, and that it was "hopelessly
romantic" in its view of the coming classless society. He said
that Marxism "betrays the ethical enterprise into an illusion,
akin to the liberal illusion." [37] He characterized it as a
religion without God or grace, but said that all "men who
live with any degree of serenity live by some assurance of
grace." [38]

In his book of 1935, *An Interpretation of Christian Ethics*,
Niebuhr tried to restate in a constructive way the relation
between politics and ethics. His disenchantment with the Social Gospel finally began to emerge as a recovery of the
doctrine of original sin, and his thought began to move in the
direction of theological anthropology. He turned to the more

distinctive insights of the Christian faith and became a theologian in a new sense. He said that "only a vital Christian faith, renewing its youth in its prophetic origin, is capable of dealing adequately with the moral and social problems of our age." [39] The question in this book was how one might move from an ethic of agape to viable ethical norms in the historical order, how "to derive a social ethic from the absolute ethic of the gospels." [40] Neither conventional orthodoxy nor liberal Christianity could give a satisfactory answer. Orthodoxy, clinging to the myths of a prescientific age, made no effort to make the Bible relevant to contemporary experience. Liberalism had surrendered the distinctives of the Christian faith in order to be modern. This book was his first broad attack on the liberal middle-class churches.

In this work Niebuhr maintained that the agape of the Cross in its sacrificial heedlessness and universalism is the only final adequate norm of human life. "The Christian doctrine of love is thus the most adequate metaphysical and psychological framework for the approximation of the ideal of love in human life." [41] He asserted that the ethic of agape is impossible to fulfill by the natural man in his historical sinful situation. He said that the "modern pulpit would be saved from much sentimentality if the thousands of sermons which are annually preached upon these texts would contain some suggestions of the impossibility of these ethical demands." [42] Agape remained as a transcendent norm, a radical perfectionism. "The ethic of Jesus may offer valuable insights to and sources of criticism for a prudential social ethic which deals with present realities; but no such social ethic can be directly derived from a pure religious ethic." [43] The ideal must transcend history since every norm that is found in history is too partial and incomplete. Man, however, tried to make the historical norm his final norm. In making absolute claims for the partial finite values, man tries to make himself God. This is the root and nature of sin. "The devil is always an angel who pretends to be God. Therefore, while egoism is the driving force of sin, dishonesty is its final expression." [44]

An Interpretation of Christian Ethics makes clear that man's tendency to claim more for himself than he ought to claim constitutes the Christian doctrine of original sin. On the one hand, Niebuhr denied the orthodox tendency to convert the doctrine of original sin into a doctrine of a literally inherited corruption. This would destroy both freedom and responsibility. On the other hand, he rejected the liberal tradition which denied that man had this tendency toward playing God. "The orthodox church dismissed the immediate relevancy of the law of love for politics. . . . The modern church approached the injustices and conflicts of this world with a gay and easy confidence." [45] Niebuhr's debates with both orthodoxy and liberalism were gradually leading him to a fundamental restatement of Christian theology.

In his book of 1937, *Beyond Tragedy,* he restated with theological richness some of the great themes of classical Christianity. "The cross, which stands at the centre of the Christian world view, reveals both the seriousness of human sin and the purpose and power of God to overcome it." [46] The Christian view sees through a sense of the tragic to a hope "beyond tragedy." Here it is evident that he was indebted to the fathers and reformers and particularly to Augustine. In later years he was to confess that he regretted not having studied the thought of Augustine earlier. "The matter is surprising because the thought of this theologian was to answer so many of my unanswered questions and to emancipate me finally from the notion that the Christian faith was in some way identical with the moral idealism of the past century." [47]

Beyond Tragedy is a collection of fifteen sermonic essays which grew out of materials that he had preached in colleges and universities, and is still perhaps the best introduction to Niebuhr. His analysis of the human situation in these sermons is much like that in *An Interpretation of Christian Ethics,* and he carries forward the proposals that he had made there. Man is fated to be mortal but he pretends not to be mortal. Because of his creativity, man pretends to be more than he actually is. This gives rise to his sinfulness. Because man is free, he can pretend to be more than he is and the consequences are that he bears responsibility for his sin. In his return to classical Christian anthropology, Niebuhr used the doctrine of original sin. But in rejecting orthodox literalism he restated the doctrine in a "radical" way: he reinterpreted the dogma in a parabolic or mythical fashion. For example, he said that man's fall is locatable in no historical Garden of Eden, but it is a way of speaking profoundly about what has happened in every man's experience. "We are deceivers, yet true in clinging to the idea of the fall as a symbol of the origin and the nature of evil in human life." [48]

AT THE SUMMIT

Niebuhr came to love the students and the classroom work at Union Seminary. He and Mrs. Niebuhr had open house almost every Thursday evening for his students, and the students would crowd into their apartment. Niebuhr loved teaching, and he never neglected it for his many outside activities and interests. Fierce in impersonal polemics, he dealt with students tenderly, and his office was never closed to them. He was the gregarious type of professor who liked to be stopped in the halls by students who wanted to talk. As one of his students said, "A lot of other professors talk about being sorry not to see more of the students. But they go off to their offices and close the door. Reinie's door is always open—and he's always being stopped in the hall by someone." [49] He thrived on the exchange with students, and missed them when he was away from the seminary.

He had a voice that carried, a burning intensity that showed in his carriage and conversation, a large frame, and the broad, thick hands of a farmer. Even when speaking casually he spoke rapidly. His hands and arms were in con-

stant motion as he preached or spoke in private conversation.
He could often be seen walking two poodles on a leash on the
streets around Union Seminary. Charming and witty in personal conversation, he was formidable as a debating opponent.
He was a 17-hour-a-day dynamo who lived a disciplined,
mildly ascetic life. His torrent of trenchant speeches and
articles were often turned out at the last minute.

Niebuhr was a tough adversary. He called pacifists "para-
sites," death-of-God theologians "infants," religious services
at the White House "complacent conformity," and, to the
end, the name "Richard Nixon" could evoke from him well-
chosen epithets. Even among friends, he was not fully at
home in any preexisting ideological camp. His opponents
were numerous. If "his ideas were too orthodox for the
liberals, they were too liberal for the orthodox; and if too
secular for the religious, they were too religious for the
secular." [50] At the same time he knew the meaning of love
and forgiveness. He was sensitive and could be hurt. When
in the wrong, he was ready to admit his error and seek forgiveness. He was keenly aware of the difference between an
attack on a person and an attack on a position. He is well
remembered for the vigorous polemic with which he could
destroy a position contrary to his own, but in his later years
he often deplored the combativeness of his earlier years.
Many felt that his main gift lay in demolition, but this was
only partially true. He negated other positions in order to
clear the ground for making his positive affirmations more
readily understood. Well aware of the falsehoods in his own
claims to truth, he tried to avoid inordinate claims for his
own position in relation to that of an opponent.

Those who knew and praised his greatness also spoke of
his "humanity" and "humility." Robert McAfee Brown, one
of Niebuhr's students, said that Niebuhr wore his national
and international honors "lightly." "It needs to be stressed,
therefore, that the man who so tellingly reacquainted a whole
theological generation with the sin of pride was himself

singularly free of that shortcoming." [51] John C. Bennett, Niebuhr's colleague at Union for many years, spoke of his tenderness. "Those who worked with him and especially his students will remember him as a person of extraordinary personal power which was expressed through his physical presence as well as through thought and word, but in so far as their personal relations with him are concerned, they will even more remember his tenderness." [52] The only student reaction Niebuhr did not know how to cope with was praise.

It was rapidly becoming obvious that Niebuhr was emerging as a commanding and brilliant voice in American theology. It came as no surprise to his colleagues when he was invited to the University of Edinburgh as the Gifford Lecturer in the spring and autumn of 1939. Only four other Americans—William James, Josiah Royce, William Ernest Hocking, and John Dewey—had been invited to give these famous lectures. Niebuhr delivered these lectures against the backdrop of the guns of World War II and the air raid sirens of Edinburgh, Scotland.

The Gifford Lectures became Niebuhr's theological masterpiece, the central achievement of his career. This effort has been called by some of his admirers the most prodigious apologia for the Christian faith ever written by an American theologian. They were published under the title *The Nature and Destiny of Man,* the first volume of which was published in 1941. This book, his longest and most important, marked the crystallization of his theology. All of his thought and writings since his Detroit pastorate had been moving toward the unifying theme of Christian selfhood. How shall man think of himself? was the opening question of his Gifford Lectures, and this question represents the core of his thought, his controlling theological principle. This book contains innumerable themes, but many have considered the phenomenology of selfhood to be the profoundest and most original theme running through it. The decisive fulcrum is the inquiry into the nature of the self. Niebuhr said, "I chose the only

subject I could have chosen because the other fields of
Christian thought were beyond my competence. I lectured on
'The Nature and Destiny of Man.' " [53]

Niebuhr's principal preoccupation was with the doctrine
of man. He stands in a great line of Christian thinkers
stretching from Augustine through Kierkegaard who have
been occupied with anthropology. For Barth and Bonhoeffer,
everything focused on Christ. For Niebuhr, Christ was utterly
important, but he had no interest in the classical formulations
of the doctrine of Christ. The doctrine of man gives body
and substance to everything in Niebuhr's rich multiplicity of
themes. He reinstated for the American intellectual community a sense of the mysterious heights and depths of man
that are possible for the Christian vision. Niebuhr holds our
attention along with the other great thinkers of our time—
such as Jaspers, Heidegger, Faulkner, Camus, and Sartre—
who have expressed the most vital vision of man.

The Nature and Destiny of Man was Niebuhr's most comprehensive and definitive theological statement. He offered a
forceful "Christian" view of man, comparing this view with
others that fail to take into account all the facts of human
existence—Greek classical views in the ancient world, and
naturalism in the modern world. Niebuhr's approach was
pronouncedly Protestant, based as it was on the Reformers,
Augustine, and the Bible. The two volumes must be considered together to get at Niebuhr's purpose. Human nature is
the created conjunction of spirit and nature. Man's sin, acted
out in the historical process, consists in man's self-centered
refusal to recognize his creaturely limits. On the other hand,
human destiny is a historical drama which begins at creation,
reaches a climax at the coming of Christ, and moves on to
conclude at Judgment Day. In this chapter I will sketch only
the barest outline of Niebuhr's book, but return to it in detail
in the following chapters.

Niebuhr began the *Nature* volume by saying that man is
a problem to himself. Both ancient and modern views of man

create problems for themselves because of their limited view-
points. When man is defined only in terms of mind, rationality, or spirit, then man's involvement in nature is neglected.
When man is defined only in terms of nature or natural process, then man's self-conscious and self-transcendent freedom
is ignored. Niebuhr said that, contrary to these two alternatives, the biblical view sees man as a unity of body and spirit,
of freedom and creatureliness. Thus a Christian view avoids
the errors and combines the truths of the alternative views of
man. Niebuhr maintained this Christian view throughout the
book. Only in God does man find the source and key to his
fulfillment. Niebuhr next analyzed non-Christian views of
man for the elements of form and vitality as well as the ideas
of individuality and collectivism. Again he argued that the
Christian view is best able to hold together in a vital balance
these contrasting aspects of man's nature.

The one pervasive trait of the many conflicting views of
modern man is their radical misreading of the nature and
extent of evil in man. Niebuhr spoke of the "easy conscience
of modern man." Modern man has rejected the traditional
Christian doctrine of original sin. Modern man has thought
well of himself and asserted that he is sufficiently intelligent
and virtuous to solve his problems and shape his destiny.
Modern man feels that any lingering evils of inertia or ignorance can be cured by social reform or education.

Niebuhr developed his biblical view of man under the idea
that man is both in the image of God, and a self-venerating
sinner. Unlike many of the early church fathers who, under
the influence of Greek philosophy, sought to identify the
image of God with human reason, Niebuhr, following Augustine, saw the image of God as the self-conscious and self-
transcendent character of man's whole self. At the same time
this free and self-determinate man is a finite, mortal creature
in God's creation. As image of God, man is both free and
finite.

Niebuhr looked upon man as essentially ambiguous. On

the one hand, man is a creature embedded in nature. On the other hand, man has the capacity to rise above his creature-hood in indeterminable acts of self-transcendence. Man is both free and bound, both limited and limitless. Alternatives to the Christian faith have either emphasized man's creature-hood or emphasized his freedom to the neglect of the other side. The biblical faith, on the other hand, emphasizes both man's creaturehood and man as being made in the image of God. Man belongs both to the realm of nature and to the realm of spirit.

As the image of God man tries "to play God"; that is, to make himself the center of all things. Man is a sinner. There is no absolute necessity for man to be self-centered for man is free to find his proper center in God. But self-centeredness is overwhelmingly probable because the tension between man's freedom and his finitude creates a situation of temp-tation. Man's sinful relation to God expresses itself as pride-ful self-deification at the individual level, while it expresses itself as injustice towards one's fellow man at the collective level. Sinful egotism is even more pronounced in groups (collective egotism) than in individuals. Group pride, which identifies itself with whatever is taken as the ultimate, con-stitutes itself as the final expression of pride. In this volume Niebuhr established his reputation as the diagnostician of sin in its subtle and blatant forms, and was to lead Emil Brunner to comment that sin was the concept that "became one of the main pillars of his thought structure." [54]

Niebuhr began his *Destiny* volume with a basic distinction between historical and nonhistorical views of man. The non-historical views either subsume history to nature or swallow it up in eternity. Historical types expect a Messiah, a figure in whom the meaning of history is fulfilled. For Niebuhr the figure of Christ fulfilled history. While Jesus fulfilled Old Testament hopes he rejected or radically reformed them when he renounced Jewish legalism and particularism. The Cross of Jesus was the climactic expression of God's decisive work to man and God's power at work reconciling man to Himself.

The Cross, God's sacrificial love for man, defined the limits and possibilities of history. Man's love is fragmentary and corrupted and needs God's sacrificial love to perfect it. Niebuhr took the Protestant view that even the regenerate man continues his sinful, egotistical behavior. The Renaissance, with its new and optimistic estimate of man, suggested that man could shape his destiny without God's gracious help. Modern man has taken his cue from the Renaissance and feels that man is both good and self-sufficient, thus rejecting the Reformation idea that man is finite, corrupt, and in need of God's grace.

Niebuhr proposed a synthesis between the Renaissance and Reformation views, an offensive element in his thought to the orthodox. He said that man in history stands before ever-new possibilities of both good and evil. The Renaissance appreciated human aspirations and the continued new possibilities of the good. The Reformation was aware of the power of sin to infect even man's best endeavors. Niebuhr pointed to two results of such a synthesis—tolerance and social justice. Man can have truth without having the final Truth. Man can believe with deep and genuine conviction without the arrogant finality or absoluteness which generates intolerance. Again, all human achievements in law and social justice can be recognized for their validity, but at the same time it can be acknowledged that they fall short of the perfection of the Kingdom of God (the ideal society). Niebuhr's Christian realism thus avoided utopian illusions and the pessimism of historical determinism. Only the Judgment at the end of history can fulfill the final meaning of history. Niebuhr ended the *Destiny* volume by saying that only eschatology can rescue the political pragmatist who seeks to keep history going with only minor adjustments in the system.

We will return to this volume in the following chapters and examine it in detail.

Before the opening salvos of World War II, Niebuhr had been writing occasional essays on various political issues. In 1940 he published sixteen of these essays in a book entitled *Christianity and Power Politics*. He said that the common thesis of the book was "that modern Christian and secular perfectionism, which places a premium upon non-participation in conflict, is a very sentimentalized version of the Christian faith and is at variance with the profoundest insights of the Christian religion." [55] Liberal perfectionism (to be good is to avoid conflict), Niebuhr held, was both bad religion and bad politics, and left America weak before Nazi tyranny. In the book's first chapter, "Why the Christian Church is not Pacifist," he argued that "the failure of the Church to espouse pacifism is not apostasy, but is derived from an understanding of the Christian Gospel which refuses simply to equate the Gospel with the 'law of love.' " [56] The American Church, however, in its efforts to keep America out of the war was "unable to help the needy for fear lest pity for the victims of tyranny imperil its precious neutrality." [57] Liberal perfectionism (in religion or politics) was unable to make significant distinctions between the peace of capitulation to tyranny and the peace of the Kingdom of God. This book was Niebuhr's warning to America not to surrender to evil whatever the alternative conflict.

The Nature and Destiny of Man emphasized the doctrines of man and history, the two doctrines where Niebuhr placed his greatest emphasis. During World War II his writing turned in another direction. He helped form and edit the journal *Christianity and Crisis*, a publication dedicated to interpreting the Christian faith in a manner relevant to the threat of tyranny. He deliberately pulled away from *Christian Century*, the journal with which he had been associated, because he felt that it was totally unrealistic in its attitude toward Hitler. He held that the threat of Hitler should be regarded as more evil than participation in a war to stop Hitler's tyranny. During the war his journalistic writings generally supported President Roosevelt's conduct of the war.

As the war came to an end, Niebuhr wrote his major treatise on democratic political theory, *The Children of Light and the Children of Darkness* (1944). It was his defense of democracy (which had so recently been under military attack), and a corrective of its traditional defense (which he felt was based on an overly optimistic estimate of man's moral capacities). He believed that a better understanding of man—neither too pessimistic nor too optimistic—would give democracy a more secure standing. One of his most quoted aphorisms states the thesis of the book: "Man's capacity for justice makes democracy possible; but man's inclination to injustice makes democracy necessary." [58]

Since man is moral—a "child of light"—he can achieve a degree of community harmony, but as basically self-serving —a "child of darkness"—his egoistic will-to-power needs to be checked. Democracy is of all systems best endowed both to guard against the misuse of power and to encourage man's benevolent side. "The children of darkness are evil because they know no law beyond the self. They are wise, though evil, because they understand the power of self-interest. The children of light are virtuous because they have some conception of a higher law than their own will. They are usually foolish because they do not know the power of self-will. They underestimate the peril of anarchy in both the national and the international community." [59] Niebuhr felt that a working democracy is a living refutation of both optimism and cynicism.

The major weakness of a democracy is its paralysis in foreign policy before a determined foe. Democratic foreign policy depends on the consensus of the nation, but this seldom comes soon enough in a crisis. With a sense of urgency Niebuhr warned that the "preservation of a democratic civilization requires the wisdom of the serpent and the harmlessness of the dove. The children of light must be armed with the wisdom of the children of darkness but remain free from their malice. They must know the power of self-interest in human society without giving it moral justification. They must have this wisdom in order that they may beguile, deflect, harness and restrain self-interest, individual and collective, for the sake of the community." [60]

Niebuhr's political philosophy was grounded in a Christian theology which he had already stated in his Gifford Lectures. He began to give ever-increasing attention to international politics after World War II.

At this stage in his career Niebuhr was becoming more influential in public life. He was appointed as an advisor to the State Department's policy planning staff. He also served as a U.S. delegate to UNESCO. As a liberal Democrat he was one of the founders of Americans for Democratic Action and at one time its chairman. He was three times Chairman of the Liberal Party in New York politics. He wrote resource materials and provided sectional leadership at the World Council of Churches in Amsterdam in 1948. He served on the National Council of Churches as a consultant on the commission to work with Secretary of State John Foster Dulles. In later years his friends sponsored a Niebuhr chair of social ethics at Union Seminary. A list of these friends is an index of his influence and includes such names as Adolph Berle, Chester Bowles, Ralph Bunche, David Dubrinsky, Norman Thomas, George Kennan, Paul Hoffman, Walter Reuther, Herbert Lehman, Walter Lippmann, Stanley Isaacs, Henry Luce, Arthur Schlesinger, Jr., Robert Oppenheimer, Eleanor Roosevelt, Beardsley Ruml, George Shuster, William Hocking, Adlai Stevenson, Charles Taft, Joseph Rauh, Hubert Humphrey and Robert Hutchins. World figures numbered in this group were Arnold Toynbee, Alan Paton, Barbara Ward, Jacques Maritain, Sir Sarvepalli Radhakrishnan, Sir Walter Moberly, W. H. Auden, and Charles Malik.[61] Association with political shapers and molders became a permanent part of his life-style. He was active in scores of organizations for particular causes.

In 1946 Niebuhr published his second book of sermonic essays (*Discerning the Signs of the Times*) elaborating the two facets of Christian hope—belief in the realization of God's will in human history and an understanding that the Christian hope transcends the limits of history. In the preface to the book, Niebuhr wrote that our age, confronted by so many hopes and frustrations, "is in particular need of the Christian gospel; and requires both the relative-historical, and the final-and-absolute facets of the Christian hope to maintain its sanity and its sense of the meaning of existence." [62]

These sermons are typical of his university preaching when he was still at his critical and polemical task and before he felt free to shift to an increasing stress on the grace of God and its power to reshape human life. He was still in the apologetic phase of his preaching—negatively analytical and critical to break down false optimism before justification by faith took place. For Niebuhr, judgment preceded mercy, and these sermons reflect more of judgment than mercy. His sermon "The City Which Hath Foundations" is typical of the others in the book. He began the sermon by saying that the Bible has both a this-worldly and an other-worldly hope. God's Kingdom is both realized and unrealized in this life. This dilemma should be accepted by faith in humility, looking to God to give final meaning to existence. Therefore, we should be faithful in our duties and cease to worry about our success in bringing in God's Kingdom. No facile resolutions of this dilemma are offered the hearer (reader) of the sermon, but the hearer is invited to go on struggling with the problem under the grace of God.

Niebuhr returned in 1949 to his formulation of a Christian theology of history. His book *Faith and History* compared Christian and modern views of history and brought out the distinctiveness of the former by contrasting it with the latter. He said this book was "but an elaboration of the second part of my Gifford Lectures." [63] The method was apologetic: the Christian view was set in opposition to the classical Greek view (meaning for history is found in a changeless realm of ideas) and the modern view (both time and history are self-explanatory). "The Christian Gospel is negatively validated by the evidence that both forms of worldly wisdom, leading to optimism and to pessimism, give an inadequate view of the total human situation." [64] Although a Christian philosophy of history cannot be rationally demonstrated, Niebuhr argued, an indirect defense is possible by showing that alternative views fail to account for all the facts of history. "The truth of the Christian faith must, in fact, be apprehended in any age by repentance and faith. It is, therefore, not made acceptable by rational validation." [65]

Niebuhr's thesis was that the gospel of Christ is true for all men and thus relevant to the historical process in all ages. The Christian view begins with the sovereignty of God in creation, judgment, and redemption. "The sovereignty of God establishes the general frame of meaning for life and history." [66] God's sovereignty is most fully disclosed in the center of historical meaning, Jesus the Christ, who reveals the divine love which transfigures historical justice and who reconciles the ambiguities of human existence. "The New Testament makes the startling claim that in Christ history has achieved both its end and a new beginning." [67] This Christian interpretation rejects the criterion of rational intelligibility as the final court of appeal in both its Greek (historical events have no significance) and modern forms (history itself is redemptive). History gets its meaning from a rationally offensive "scandal of particularity"—the event of one who is received and acclaimed as the Christ.

God's lordship over history most clearly denies the "wisdom of the world" in two decisive movements—the crucifixion and resurrection of Jesus. These two events climax all previous revelations, disclose God's unique relationship to man, elucidate the dramas of sin and redemption as they unfold in history, and point to the end of history where God will give history its final meaning. "This pinnacle of faith in New Testament religion is the final expression of certainty about the power of God to complete our fragmentary life as well as the power of His love to purge it of the false completions in which all history is involved." [68] Thus Niebuhr once again argued against both the utopian dreams of those who sought to flee from the historical process into a timeless realm and those who were too optimistic in their interpretation of history.

Niebuhr quickly moved to another volume on history as the post-World War II years saw his attention turn to international politics. He turned to irony as the major motif of his interpretation of history in *The Irony of American History* (1952). The book marks his movement politically toward pragmatic liberalism of the Franklin D. Roosevelt type, and philosophically toward irony rather than tragedy in his philosophy of history. Both shifts in his thinking indicated that he was less dogmatic in his approach to history than he had been in his Gifford Lectures and more open to human accomplishment.

Niebuhr said, "Irony consists of apparently fortuitous incongruities in life which are discovered, upon closer examination, to be not merely fortuitous." [69] The biblical interpretation of human history rejects the pathetic (the pain caused by unthinking natural evil) and the tragic (a conscious choice of evil for the sake of good) for the ironic (evil resulting from man's wrong use of his unique capacities). When hidden vanities or pretensions are exposed, then the irony of a situation is disclosed and tends to be cured. Thus Niebuhr turned to the pretensions of virtue, wisdom, and power in American life in order to confront America with its ironies and free it of its illusions in the conduct of foreign policy. He said that American civilization "is involved in many ironic refutations of its original pretensions of virtue, wisdom, and power." [70] He claimed that this approach was theological because irony was the normative way for Christians to view history. God "laughs at human pretensions without being hostile to human aspirations," he

said.[71] He hoped by pointing out America's ironies to dis-
solve them and reduce America's pretensions without destroying America's faith in its future. He said that America
looked upon itself as the most innocent nation upon earth:
"The irony of our situation lies in the fact that we could not
be virtuous (in the sense of practicing the virtues which are
implicit in meeting our vast world responsibilities) if we
were really as innocent as we pretend to be." [72]

Niebuhr continued his major role at Union Seminary,
eventually being appointed vice-president. His life-style of
"Christian realism" began to produce a new breed of church
leader. Churchmen were influenced by one or more of his
themes. "Representative of these various types were men like
Roger L. Shinn, who succeeded Niebuhr at Union in the chair
of Applied Christianity; George William Webber, founder
of the East Harlem Protestant Parish and later president of
New York Biblical Seminary; Truman Douglass, leading
spirit in the affairs of the National Council of Churches and
pioneer in church involvement in human issues; and Martin
Luther King, Jr." [73] Niebuhr was at the apex of his influence
in the early 1950s and was to remain there for over a decade
longer.

THE LATER YEARS

Niebuhr's robust health began to fade in the period after
World War II. In 1952 he had a heart attack which slowed
but did not stop his activity. After retirement from Union
Theological Seminary in 1960 to continue his theological and
political concerns, he was invited to study at the Institute for
Advanced Studies at Princeton, and he was active in the
Center for the Study of Democratic Institutions at Santa
Barbara, California. He moved to his retirement home at
Yale Hill in Stockbridge, Massachusetts, in 1966. A series
of strokes sapped his energy and gradually paralyzed him
over the last twenty years of his life. He underwent lengthy

hospitalization and had to reduce his activities for months at a time. Eventually he regained his speech and some arm movement, but he was unable to travel freely.

He bore his life of sharp physical pain with grace and humor, but his severe limitations caused difficulties for his family and friends. The companionship and help of his wife, Ursula, were of inestimable value during his long convalescence. He became frail and husbanded his strength for those moments when a speech had to be given. He continued to write on a restricted schedule and to entertain friends at his Stockbridge home together with Mrs. Niebuhr. The deep and warm personal and interpersonal life he had cultivated in earlier years sustained him in his time of weakness. Being an invalid deepened his understanding of himself, the Bible, and prayer.

Christian Realism and Political Problems (1953) was a book of essays on theological, ethical, and political themes that Niebuhr published during his illness. The essays said nothing that he had not already said in principle, but they do reflect a new awareness and indebtedness to the political realism of St. Augustine. Niebuhr held that Augustine's value for the Christian political thinker lay in the interpretation of human selfhood which enabled Augustine to "view the heights of human creativity and the depths of human destructiveness, which avoids the errors of moral sentimentality and cynicism, and their alternate corruptions of political systems of both secular and Christian thinkers." [74] Out of the emotional depression coming from his physical illness Niebuhr searched anew and more deeply into the meaning of human selfhood. *The Self and the Dramas of History* (1955) reflects his thinking at this time and is a further development of his phenomenology of selfhood.

The Self and the Dramas of History is an excellent example of Niebuhr's spiritual fortitude. He said that it was "written in two years of enforced leisure." Actually, the "leisure" was a severe illness that would have put most of us in a home for incurables. This book is a splendid tribute to a sick man who refused to be a passive patient. When the worst of his illness was over he began to write down this book and develop a theme already implicit in his earlier works. This is probably his third most important book. The self is a difficult and omnipresent problem, and he handled it in such a way that the practical implications of some very intricate theological constructions became persuasively clear.

This book also demonstrates Niebuhr's genius for timeliness. He always had an instinct for the heart of the emerging great issues. He did it first with *Moral Man and Immoral Society* when he pointed out the tragic discrepancy between the personal and the social dimensions of ethical behavior. The ripeness of the idea made the book a turning point in American theology. Later, when he focused on man as sinner in the first volume of his Gifford Lectures (*The Nature of Man*), he did it again, and this study of man's alienation from God, self, and society became a modern classic. His treatment of man as sinner became widely familiar even to those who did not read Niebuhr himself. In *The Self and the Dramas of History* Niebuhr, for the third time, grasped the ripeness of a great idea and found a means to give it common understanding. He had long explored the complexities of human nature in history and society, but in this book he turned the problem around and looked at the subject which was involved, turning from the objective self which most analysts look at to the subjective self behind the object.

In 1952 Paul Tillich published *The Courage To Be*, in which he said that man discovers himself when he discovers his existence is in the structure of "being itself." Tillich put his emphasis on ontology, which meant for him that ontology was prior to ethics. Niebuhr and Tillich, although good friends and closely allied in many a cause, had very different theological styles. In *The Self and the Dramas of History* Niebuhr returned to the debate about man's nature and freedom, and this book may be read as Niebuhr's public reply

to Tillich. Niebuhr objected to Tillich's use of ontological
categories because he felt that such categories curtailed man's
freedom through their rigidity. Hence Niebuhr defined the
self in terms of its dialogues rather than in terms of its structure of being or its participation in the structure of being:
"The self is a creature which is in constant dialogue with
itself, with its neighbors, and with God, according to the
Biblical viewpoint." [75] He held that the self, its communities,
and its experience of love should be interpreted in dramatic
historical categories rather than in terms of ontological fate.

Niebuhr illustrated, with great penetration and force, the
truth that the human self cannot be its own end. Whenever
the self is devoted to its own self-realization it fails. It is
only as a person gives himself over to the power and grace
of God that true selfhood is realized. The most important
part of the book (part 1) deals with the self in its three
dialogues—with its own self, with others, and with God.

The self can only be defined in terms of its three inter-
actions. It is much more complicated than either "mind" or
"body" or any of the conventional categories for defining it.
The self in dialogue with itself "is an empiric fact in the
sense that every astute person must admit that such a dialogue
goes on in the internal life of the self, though there are no
external evidences of this dialogue." [76] The self in dialogue
with others "is dependent upon them for the image which it
has of itself and for the spiritual security which is as necessary to the self as its social security." [77] To deny the self's
dialogue with God would be to fail in defining the total
anatomy of human selfhood. In part 2 Niebuhr sketched the
relations of selfhood and history in ancient, medieval, and
modern thought. In part 3 he applied the biblical notion of
the self he had developed in part 1 to the current social and
political order. This remarkable book is a tribute to Niebuhr's genius and the best available statement of the psychological core of his thinking.

Despite the strokes that gradually were paralyzing him,

Niebuhr continued to write topical essays. In the years
1956–57 he wrote a number of journalistic essays which
were published in 1958 as *Pious and Secular America.* They
are dated, as all journalism is. Their unity is found in Niebuhr's interest in relating Christianity to the social and
political life of America. Niebuhr continued in this book to
reveal to Americans the ironies in our history, to point up
the incongruities between America's myths and America's
realities.

> We are "religious" in the sense that religious communities enjoy
> the devotion and engage the active loyalty of more laymen than in
> any nation of the Western world. We are "secular" in the sense
> that we pursue the immediate goals of life, without asking too
> many ultimate questions about the meaning of life and without
> being too disturbed by the tragedies and antinomies of life.[78]

For Niebuhr one of the chief ironies was that America was
superior to the communists in the pursuit of happiness, not
because of America's piety, but because of America's secular,
scientific, and technical proficiency. He observed that "our
'Godly materialism' has been immeasurably more successful
than their 'godless' variety." [79]

Niebuhr's major and most formal work on political theory,
The Structure of Nations and Empires (1959), tried to distinguish the contingent from the permanent in international
politics. He deliberately tried to isolate the perennial features of imperialism, and he argued that there are discernible
patterns by which strong nations relate to weak nations. He
said the fact that the American and Russian "empires," the
two postwar superpowers, tried to establish hegemonic relationships over other nations is *the* most important feature of
the international system. He said that it is probable "that the
world will live, if it does not destroy itself, for a long time
in a state of semi-anarchy in which certain centers of authority, power, and prestige will mitigate the anarchy much
as anarchy was mitigated in nineteenth century Europe by
the balance of power." [80]

Niebuhr found in Western history a recurring pattern in which strong nations exercised power over weaker nations. He felt that this pattern was inevitable and the moral results ambiguous—both harmful and beneficial. After tracing the long history of conflict between communities both national and imperial, he concluded that the struggle had "reached a climax in the cold war and the nuclear dilemma of the present day." [81] Further, the climax "certainly contradicts and refutes most of the philosophies of history in which the wise men of two previous centuries attempted to chart the course of history and to predict its future." [82]

Niebuhr was trying to make Christian moral claims relevant to international politics, so in the book he turned specifically in his application to the problems the United States faced in the cold war. He hoped to show that America was not as virtuous in her foreign policy as she supposed, nor the Soviet Union as evil as Americans supposed she was. Speaking of America's relation to Russia in the cold war, he said, "The task of managing to share the world without bringing disaster on a common civilization must include, on our part, a less rigid and self-righteous attitude toward the power realities of the world and a more hopeful attitude toward the possibilities of internal developments in the Russian despotism." [83] Niebuhr concluded his study with the warning that he had voiced years before in his Gifford Lectures, that human freedom entailed both creative and destructive features: "It is creative when an ultimate norm or value is set in judgment over the historically relative and ambiguous achievements of man's existence. It is destructive and a source of evil if a simple identification is made between the ultimate norm and the norms and values which we cherish." [84] The only safe way to build a cold-war community was to assume that the dominion which the world needs for its peace always is ambiguous morally.

Niebuhr continued to prick American illusions and point out the ironies of American history in two other books he jointly authored, one with Alan Heimert (*A Nation So Con-*

ceived, 1963) and the other with Paul E. Sigmund (*The Democratic Experience*, 1969). In both books Niebuhr argued that history was not tragic and did not of necessity end in evil. Man was destructive, but he also had creative possibilities as a free creature.

In the first book, with Heimert, Niebuhr warned America not to be too proud: "The inclination is to attribute the growth in power to our democratic virtues." [85] But characteristically he went on to praise America for its democracy: "Democracy is an ultimate norm of political organization in the sense that no better way has been found to check the inordinacy of the powerful on the one hand and the confusion of the multitude on the other than by making every center of power responsible to the people whom it affects." [86] In tracing America's growth from simple agrarian nation to complex industrial power, Niebuhr pointed out that America was responding to a sense of mission. Then he observed that the vision of the mission should keep us from "nostalgic yearning after the original simplicities, for the sake of fleeing or avoiding present complexities." [87]

In the second book, with Sigmund, he reflected on the broader democratic experience of Europe and the three constant prerequisites of free governments (community solidarity, freedom of the individual, and social justice), but he continued to warn Americans of the complacency, sentimentality, utopianism, and parochialism which he saw in our heritage. He put it in Winston Churchill's words when he said, "We believe that democracy is the worst form of government on earth except for all others ever tried." [88] Niebuhr reaffirmed his "pessimistic faith" in the democratic idea, but he concluded that democracies in the emerging third world will remain an ideal more often than an operative reality.

The Nature and Destiny of Man was Niebuhr's most systematic theological statement about man. The publication in 1965 of *Man's Nature and His Communities* brought together the attempts to revise his approach that he had been making since he gave the Gifford Lectures. The new book, a collection of three essays, did not mark the breaking of any new ground nor a summing up of his work (in spite of the book's claim to the contrary). Discussing man's inhumanity to man, he examined the paradox of universalist aspirations side by side with a history of communal conflicts. He also reflected about the mixture of self-seeking and self-giving in man's selfhood and gave as well a critical survey of idealist and realist political theories. For most Niebuhr-watchers, however, the rather autobiographical introduction was of most interest. The introduction was entitled "Changing Perspectives" and represented in certain respects a revision of his views. The primary difference between this volume and the Gifford Lectures was the absence of a theological vocabulary. It was a shift away from the language of orthodox theology which offended the intellectual community. This represented a change in style but not in content.

The Nature and Destiny of Man used the theological categories of image of God, original sin, original righteousness, grace, the Kingdom of God, and the last judgment. *Man's Nature and His Communities* was Niebuhr's attempt to describe again the human situation in the light of the criticism by political philosophers of his religious language in the Gifford Lectures. On his abandonment of the term "original sin" Niebuhr wrote:

> I made a rather unpardonable pedagogical error in *The Nature and Destiny of Man*, which I hope I have corrected in the present volume. My theological preoccupation prompted me to define the persistence and universality of man's self-regard as "original sin." This was historically and symbolically correct. But my pedagogical error consisted in seeking to challenge modern optimism with the theological doctrine which was anathema to modern culture.[89]

Niebuhr admitted that he had tried to purge the doctrine of original sin of some of its cruder traditional interpretations, but this effort proved vain for his modern readers. He

learned that his readers who were political philosophers and
in substantial agreement with positions taken in his Gifford
Lectures were careful to state their disagreement with his
"theological presuppositions." Niebuhr went on to say that
Man's Nature and His Communities would "understandably
use more sober symbols of describing well-known facts." [90]
He said that he had changed his vocabulary but not his
analysis, and remarked that he still thought that the *London
Literary Times Supplement* was correct when it observed
that the "doctrine of original sin is the only empirically
verifiable doctrine of the Christian faith." [91] So Niebuhr retained his emphasis on man's freedom, sin, sacrificial love,
and God's grace, vindicating their meaning by an analysis
of contemporary history and experience.

Niebuhr demonstrated gradual but significant changes in
his outlook as his fifty-year writing career progressed. There
was no climactic change of direction such as Karl Barth's,
but he moved in response to intellectual inquiries and public
events. Over the years he gradually developed a new appreciation for certain secular disciplines and values. He said of
the essays in *Man's Nature and His Communities*:

> They also embody increasingly the insights of the secular disciplines
> and reflect the author's increasing enthusiasm for the virtues of an
> open society which allows freedom to all religious traditions, and
> also the freedom to analyze and criticize all these traditions through
> the disciplines of an empirical and historical culture.[92]

For example, he mentioned particularly the psychology of
Erik Erikson as having helped him clarify his own doctrine
of faith. Again, he had put more emphasis in his latter years
on "common grace," the "hidden Christ" operating through
ordinary human relationships. The "hidden Christ" had only
been in the footnotes of his earlier writings, but had become
a major theme of his later work. Further, he underscored
his increasing sympathy, as a Protestant, with both the Jewish
and the Catholic traditions.

The assistance of his wife, Ursula, should be noted here. For years she had edited his work and informed his writing. Niebuhr said that eventually her contributions to his work were indistinguishable from his, although they were very real. But most of all she loved him, and nursed and protected him during his years of illness.

This last Niebuhr book disclosed a mellower Niebuhr who saw that, despite the danger of sinful self-assertion, man still needed a healthy self-regard. But his topical essays continued to pour out to the end with a hard-headed, pragmatic realism. In his years of declining health, younger liberal theologians had grown up who were infected with a revolutionary, third-world "romanticism." Niebuhr warned that the poor, the weak, and the despised of yesterday might, on gaining a social victory over their oppressors, exhibit the same kind of prideful arrogance.

This remained Niebuhr's typical realism in human affairs. His last two articles in *Christianity and Crisis* in 1969 and 1970, typed out while he was in pain and fatigue, showed him alert and still polemical. One was a withering blast on White House religion ("The King's Chapel and the King's Court") and another on presidential despotism in Viet Nam ("The Presidency and the Irony of American History"). The first article reviewed the semiestablishment of religion of the first Nixon administration with the Sunday service in the East Room of the White House. Niebuhr wondered if the White House clergy were not guilty of perpetuating complacency through a failure to realize that all governments stand under God's absolute standards of justice. Although mellower, he still thrived on controversy. ·

The increasingly frail Niebuhr had a peace and serenity as he entered into death. By December of 1970 he no longer had physical strength or mental energy. No one was better prepared than he to confront the end of history that is the promise of death. He had faced eternity in every moment and in every action of his life. He knew the limitations of man but

was more persuaded of the power of God's grace to transcend
these limitations. On May 31 of the following year he died
at the age of seventy-eight in his home in Stockbridge.

Three years after Reinhold's death, Mrs. Niebuhr published a book of his sermons and prayers. "We preachers"
was how Niebuhr regarded himself, and almost every Sunday
for more than fifty years followed this vocation in the parish
and then increasingly in university and college chapels in
different parts of the country. This book represents the expression of two aspects of his ministry—to proclaim the basic
forms of the Christian faith and to relate them to social concerns. Niebuhr had said, "I am a preacher and I like to
preach." But his sermons were devoted to an analysis of the
human situation that discussed both the levels of human possibilities and the levels of human sin. Niebuhr felt that the
preacher's twofold task was to get in contact with the biblical
tradition (including the liturgical traditions of all the Christian churches) and then apply it relevantly to the special
problems, personal and social, of his people. Mrs. Niebuhr
says that her husband saw the preacher's task as showing the
relevance of the Christian faith to life, in both its individual
and social dimensions. She said that for Reinhold the Christian faith was "a present fact, and a present truth about life
that illumines our existence and gives meaning, relieves us
of some of the miseries of guilt in which all men are involved, . . . [and] explains the curious paradox of human
freedom and human necessity." [93]

If triviality and simple moral absolutes were the two besetting sins of the preacher, then relevance and applicability
were the two preacher qualities that Niebuhr most admired
and tried to emulate. Thus his ministry ended as it had begun—as a preacher and a pastor.

II. Existential Anthropology

Niebuhr never attempted to explicate all Christian theology. His system finds its beginning in the doctrine of man, and other doctrines are dealt with by indirection. This doctrine, his chief contribution to theology, is determinative for his ethics, his view of history, his Christology, his doctrine of the atonement, and his eschatology. But he understood that man is not an isolated doctrine unrelated to the total Christian faith. He dedicated his writings to the subject of man although he was a number of years arriving at his full view. He finally worked out his maturest statement in *The Nature and Destiny of Man*, and his later writings did not essentially modify that position (they were largely amplifications of it). His Gifford Lectures are one of the most important treatments of the doctrine of man in contemporary theology. His friendly critics say that Niebuhr's work on man excels anything American theology has hitherto produced. His unfriendly critics say that to read him with understanding is to reject him. Still, anyone who has failed to take account of this two-volume work has not attempted fairly to understand the present religious situation.

The following pages are my effort to state within excep-
tionally small scope certain features of Niebuhr's anthropology. I will do violence to his thought by vast omissions
and by simply not coming to grips with some of his crucial
ideas. But my hope is to point you to Niebuhr's own writings:
there is no substitute for reading him yourself. Since all the
streams of Niebuhr's previous thinking came together in *The
Nature and Destiny of Man*, I will turn most frequently to
this work.

THE PROBLEM OF MAN

Niebuhr tried to distinguish his Christian view of man
from all secular views by his interpretation of three contradictory aspects of the human situation. First, he emphasized
that man's self-transcendence in his spiritual nature is the
biblical doctrine of the "image of God." Second, he said that
man is finite, dependent, and involved in nature, yet this
finitude is not the source of evil. Third, he said evil in man
is a consequence of man's inevitable but not necessary unwillingness to accept his finitude and admit his insecurity.
We will look at the first two distinctives in this chapter, and
turn to Niebuhr's doctrine of sin in the next chapter.

Niebuhr said that man, the "existing" individual, has the
capacity to explore his environment and grasp its reality.
But the relation of the dynamic self to its environment poses
a basic problem: Is the self to be completely identified with
its environment of the natural world, or does it transcend its
environment? If the self is identical with the natural world,
then it is no more than one of the animals. If the self completely transcends the natural world, it is absorbed into a
timeless eternity. The self, as it inevitably searches for meaning in its contradictory environment, has unfortunately
grasped three premature solutions in its anxiety. According
to Niebuhr, naturalism loses the self by reducing it to the
"mechanical proportions" of nature; idealism loses the self

in the abstract universalities of mind; romanticism loses the self to the larger social collective.

The self, in a mysterious way, is both in and above its environment. As a part of nature man is a physical creature; as a part of eternity he is a free spirit. Niebuhr said, "One might define this total environment most succinctly as one which includes both eternity and time." [1] The essential man must be measured in terms of both these environments. This contradiction has always been man's most vexing problem, and his reflection upon it has consistently landed him in contradictory affirmations. Both sides of man's nature are usually not appreciated with equal sympathy, said Niebuhr. The tendency of anthropologists is to emphasize one aspect of man's nature at the expense of the other, and thus become involved in miscalculations. No simple scheme is adequate.[2] Niebuhr tried to do justice to both aspects of the self by showing that nature and spirit form the double environment in which man lives. This is the first of a number of paradoxes that he used to describe his understanding of man.

The self has its natural limitations, its forms and boundaries. Man is limited ("creaturely") by the very fact that he *is* a body. At the same time there are other aspects of man's existence which are as real as his involvement in nature. Man is unique when compared with the animals because man is the only animal who can transcend himself. The self is endowed with a freedom that enables it to transcend the limitations and necessities of nature. When the self recognizes and admits its natural limitations and physical necessities, the transition from limitation to spiritual freedom is made.

Niebuhr distinguished several levels of the self's freedom: (1) There is the self's awareness of transcending the natural process, of standing outside of nature. Man manifests this as a tool-making animal. (2) A higher level includes man's ability to make general rational concepts and his awareness of this ability. With this ability man not only transcends nature, but the world. (3) Another height of transcendence goes beyond this conceptual consciousness to self-consciousness, where man stands outside of himself. Self-consciousness is the height of man's spirit; here the self faces boundless freedom and God.

Niebuhr, prompted by Martin Buber's book *I and Thou*, stressed the freedom of self-transcendence of the self by emphasizing the three types of dialogue in which the self is involved. Niebuhr said that although there is no external evidence of the dialogue of the self with itself, every astute person knows it as an "empiric" fact. The internal dialogue of the self with itself means that the self in one of its aspects is using conceptual images to make another of its aspects its object of thought. The dialogue of the self with various neighbors takes place on endless levels, depending upon the neighbor to bring it to completion. The self is also in dialogue with God, a realm beyond limits of empirical verification. The dialogue of the self with God finds God as Judge and as Redeemer.

Man is an essential unity although he is *in* and *beyond* nature. Niebuhr divided the self into nature, rationality, and freedom of spirit for the sake of analysis. These elements in the self do not imply that the self is a trichotomy. The self is a unity. Once Niebuhr had arrived at and accepted the logical inconsistency of this multidimensional unity of man, he was remarkably consistent in maintaining the view. He is responsible for the now-famous phrase in theology that man "lives at the juncture of nature and spirit."

Niebuhr's existential interpretation of the mystery of human selfhood was informed by the nineteenth-century Danish thinker Sören Kierkegaard. Niebuhr said that Kierkegaard had interpreted the human self more accurately than any modern (and most previous) Christian theologians or psychologists. Kierkegaard's doctrine was attractive to Niebuhr because it took into account man's dialectical position between time and eternity, man's transcendence and finitude, and man's "image of God" and his corruption.

The concept of self-transcendence and the infinite outreach of memory into this self-transcendence (an idea borrowed by Niebuhr from Augustine's analysis of the phenomenon of memory) is of the greatest importance for his system of theology. The concept of a transcendence beyond rationality paves the way for a biblical revelation that is not disclosed by an analysis of human experience. Niebuhr took with equal seriousness both man's involvement in, and his transcendence over, the processes of nature. This stress on the essential unity of man was the crux of Niebuhr's position. He resorted to paradox to describe the functions of this unity because his position drove him to a logical impasse.

THE LOSS OF THE SELF IN IDEALISM, NATURALISM, AND ROMANTICISM

Two sources for Niebuhr's basic presuppositions about the nature of man have been indicated in a preliminary way in the preceding pages: the Christian revelation and an analysis of the human situation. These two sources interpenetrate each other on every level of interpretation. In his analysis of culture, Niebuhr found that the non-Christian anthropologies have variously distorted the two elements in man's nature. One side of the self is always sacrificed at the expense of the other. Either the self's natural limitations or the self's spiritual freedom receives an overemphasis.

According to Niebuhr, modern non-Christian anthropologies—a curious and unstable blend of classical and biblical views—have produced several varieties of difficulties and confusions: (1) The relation of vitality (spiritual self-transcendence) and form (the laws and limitations of nature) has caused an endless debate between naturalistic and idealistic rationalists. (2) This debate has been further complicated by the protest of the romantic naturalists against the emphasis of these rationalists. (3) The concept of individuality has been lost by modern culture. The Christian faith roots

man's individuality in his relationship to God because he is
created in the image of God. Modern culture, trying to liberate man through the "infinite possibility of the human spirit,"
has lost the self in this abortive attempt. (4) Modern culture
has tried to explain away the problem of evil, flying in the
face of the known facts of history. This optimism has led
modern culture to a philosophy of history expressed in the
idea of progress.

Niebuhr said that the modern view of man has produced
these four areas of difficulty because it offers too simple a
solution to man's dialectical nature. Modern culture ("Western" culture since the Renaissance) "is to be credited with
the greatest advances in the understanding of nature and
with the greatest confusions in the understanding of man." [3]

Idealism (as derived from Kant and Hegel) emphasizes
man's rational freedom at the expense of natural involvement, practically identifying man's reason with God. In idealism the rational man is the real man.[4] Naturalism, on the
other hand (as expressed in Francis Bacon and Montaigne),
seeks to understand man in terms of his relation to nature,
identifying man primarily as the physical man. Naturalism
reduced the human ego to a stream of consciousness in which
personal identity was at a minimum.[5] Idealism identified
consciousness with mind and finally identified the mind with
some sort of divinity or absolute. But modern culture, not
fully satisfied with either approach, sought a third answer in
romantic naturalism (rooted in Rousseau and Christian
Pietism).[6]

The protest of this newest of modern anthropologies has
taken various forms. One aspect, culminating in Nietzsche's
nihilism, is the assertion of nature's vitalities against the
peril of loss of energy through rational discipline. Another
aspect, as in Freud and Marx, is the insight that reason is
dishonest when it claims mastery over nature. A third aspect,
seen in Bergson and Schopenhauer, disputes reason's claim
to be the organizing principle of life. Yet another aspect of

this revolt, a brand of modern existentialism, ends in a deification of the self as its own creator and end.

Modern culture sensed that naturalism did not comprehend the self-transcendent human spirit, and that idealism lost spirit when it did not conform to the pattern of rationality. Spirit was annihilated through either deification or abasement. Niebuhr said that the history of modern culture began as a debate between those who explained man in terms of his reason or in terms of his relation to nature. But, he said, "the latter history of this culture is not so much a debate between these two schools of thought as a rebellion of romanticism, materialism and psychoanalytic psychology against the errors of rationalism, whether idealistic or naturalistic, in its interpretation of human nature." [7] Romantic naturalism has denied the claim of idealism that freedom and rationality are synonymous; it has also denied the claim of naturalism that the essence of man is mechanical nature. Romanticism tried to save man by stressing his vitality, claiming this could be done if man asserted himself with passionate inwardness. The result has been an autonomous individual with no checks on his self-expression. When a check is found in the state, for example, it does away with the newly won selfhood. The check becomes more important than the self.

According to Niebuhr's analysis, romanticism errs in the contradictory criticism it levels at rationalism. Romanticism charges rationalism "with the enervation on the one hand and the accentuation of natural vitalities on the other; with the creation of too broad and too narrow forms for the expression of the will-to-live or the will-to-power." [8] It errs again in its interpretation of the vitality of man when it ascribes to the biological what obviously belongs to the creativity of the spirit.[9] Freudianism makes this error when it explains man's complex spiritual phenomena in terms of biological sexual impulses. Marxism does the same thing in materialistic rather than biological terms when it ascribes vitality to the drives of the social classes. These errors indicated to Niebuhr romanticism's failure to penetrate to the paradox of the human spirit.[10] He maintained that the individual self cannot be contained within the presuppositions of any of these three competing anthropologies.

Absolute idealism admits man's transcendence over nature; and it has the advantage over naturalism in its appreciation of the depth of the human spirit. Idealism will not admit, however, that man transcends his reason; consequently, it equates the individual self with the "Absolute" and loses individuality in the universal spirit.[11] The self then becomes only an aspect of the universal mind, the cosmic reason. Idealism discounts the individuality that depends upon the particularity of the body. The naturalistic portion of modern culture strips the self of transcendence and reduces it to a stream of consciousness.[12] When man is identified with the natural order, when time becomes everything, when history is self-explanatory, individuality is lost. Niebuhr said that this philosophy runs throughout the modern capitalistic, bourgeois pattern of life. Romanticism tried to save individuality by giving it unqualified significance. It emphasized the essence of man as feeling, imagination, and will. It ignored the norm of reason or the norm of God and absolutized each individual instead. But romanticism eventually recoiled from this self-glorification (all but Nietzsche) and replaced the individual with a collective individual such as the state or nation. The collective individual then became the center of existence. Niebuhr said that this is the cultural history of modern nationalism.[13]

In summary, Niebuhr said that individuality, the most unique emphasis of modern culture, cannot be maintained within the presuppositions of modern culture.

In idealism the individual is able to transcend the tyrannical necessities of nature only to be absorbed in the universalities of impersonal mind. In the older naturalism, the individual is able for a moment to appreciate that aspect of individuality which the variety of natural circumstances creates; but true individuality is quickly lost because nature knows nothing of the self-transcendence, self-identity and freedom which are the real marks of individuality. In romantic naturalism the individuality of the person is quickly subordinated to the unique and self-justifying individuality of the social collective. Only in Nietzschean romanticism is the individual preserved; but there he becomes the vehicle of daemonic religion because he knows no law but his own will-to-power and has no God but his own unlimited ambition.[14]

Using this criticism, Niebuhr negated these competing anthropologies. He maintained that Christianity can give a vantage point which presents a proper balance of both freedom and involvement. In the history of thought the Christian emphasis on individuality is best expressed in the Reformation doctrine of the priesthood of all believers. "Without the presuppositions of the Christian faith," said Niebuhr, "the individual is either nothing or becomes everything." [15] Niebuhr held that Christianity accepts all that is valid in the presuppositions of modern culture, but does not fall prey to its errors.

Niebuhr also criticized idealism, naturalism, and romanticism for their optimistic treatment of evil. He wrote that man's sinfulness is universally rejected by contemporary culture; the Christian account of man's sinfulness is discarded as irrelevant. Idealism finds the root of evil in man's involvement in nature, and hopes to free him by increasing his rational faculties. On the other hand, naturalism and romanticism hope to overcome evil by a return to the harmony and unity of nature.

An easy conscience is the unifying force among the competing anthropologies of modern culture, and they justify this by the most diverse and contradictory metaphysical theories. Evidence to the contrary, said Niebuhr, does not seem to disturb man's good opinion of himself. Modern man views himself in only one dimension (either nature or reason) and attempts to derive evil from some specific historical source such as religion (Holbach and Helvetius), autocratic government (Hobbes, Locke, and Adam Smith), or economic organization (Marx).

Idealism has a simpler approach to the problem of evil in

history than does naturalism. Idealism recognizes the presence
of evil in history, but it makes a distinction between nature
and reason and attributes evil to the body.[16] Idealism is
complacent about the perils of the freedom of the human
spirit, convinced that spirit and rationality are identical and
that rationality controls freedom. Naturalism and romanticism, on the other hand, believe that they can easily return
to the innocency of nature. Naturalism looks upon man as
essentially good, and advocates a return to the harmony of
nature as the way of salvation (Rousseau, John Dewey). This
optimistic approach to man's virtue and the problem of evil
expresses itself philosophically as the idea of progress in
history.[17] The empirical method of modern culture has been
successful in understanding nature; but, when applied to an
understanding of human nature, it was blind to some obvious
facts about human nature that simpler cultures apprehended
by the wisdom of common sense.

In this cultural approach to the doctrine of man, Niebuhr
found that all contemporary non-Christian views of life fail
because they do not fully take into account man's freedom on
the one hand or his involvement in nature on the other. In
pointing out the self-refuting qualities of alternate explana-
tions, he hoped to pave the way for the relevance of the
Christian explanation.

Niebuhr's treatment of idealism, naturalism, and romanticism in his cultural analysis was typical of his approach to
a problem.

> A somewhat stylized Niebuhrian analysis of a human problem is
> to state two opposite facets of the problem, then to reduce each
> further to negative and positive elements, to correlate the subnega-
> tion, then to show how the Christian answer meets these complexi-
> ties, but only in the wholeness of the problem; for once any element
> of the Christian answer is emphasized at the expense of some other
> facet, distortion occurs.[18]

Niebuhr's belief that the deeper truths about man must be
stated in such a way as to include the contradictory aspects

of reality was an offense to many. This is a self-contradictory position to the rationalists, especially when Niebuhr did not give a synthesis to the thesis-antithesis nature of reality. Many secular positions would be destroyed if they admitted the full complexity that Niebuhr pointed up. This "relational" or "dialectical" pattern of thought, Niebuhr maintained, is well adapted to the complexity of life and to the Christian answer to it. This pattern of thought sometimes became mechanical; this was to be expected in any stylized pattern that tried to deal with the varying aspects of reality.

RESOURCES FROM THE CHRISTIAN FAITH

The first source for Niebuhr's doctrine of man was an analysis of culture. His second source was the Christian revelation. Although the analysis of culture preceded his exposition of the Christian answer to the problem of man, his analysis of culture presupposed the acceptance of the Christian faith. For Niebuhr there was no inquiry into the human situation without a faith presupposition. To attempt an exposition of the doctrine of man outside the context of the Christian faith would oversimplify the human situation. Niebuhr said that modern culture does not have a principle of interpretation that adequately takes into account the unity of man's self-transcendence and his physical life, the meaning of individuality, or the origin of evil.[19]

Niebuhr defined man's total environment as including both time and eternity. He maintained that the Christian revelation does not reduce man to nature, nor absorb him into an undifferentiated eternity. Christianity answers the problem of man with its doctrines of man as made in the image of God and man as creature. These doctrines are also the key to man's individuality. Further, Christianity answers the problem of evil with its doctrine of original sin.

Niebuhr, wary of traditional epistemology because reason is usually assumed to be the key that understands the form or structure of unity that encompasses the self, linked himself with the dramatic and historical method of the Bible. He expressed it this way: "My point is simply that when we deal with aspects of reality which exhibit a freedom above and beyond structures, we must resort to the Hebraic dramatic and historical way of apprehending reality. Both the divine and the human self belong to this category." [20] The biblical insight rests upon the encounter in freedom between the self and God beyond the limits of philosophy. Niebuhr's thought, inseparable from his religious faith, drew upon the Bible for its basic insights. He ran into constant criticism, however, for the way in which he handled the biblical testimony. The chief reason for this criticism was that Niebuhr considered myth to be the primary language of the Bible in its description of the dynamic nature of history (both its beginning and its end) and the encounter of the self with God in freedom.

Niebuhr regretted that he had used the term *myth* (and the term is perhaps unfortunate, as myth implies a fairy tale to most people). But by myth he meant that which, although it temporarily deceived, nonetheless pointed to a truth that could only be expressed in that form. Niebuhr said, "The word has subjective and skeptical connotations. I am sorry I ever used it, particularly since the project for 'demythologizing' the Bible has been undertaken and bids fair to reduce the Biblical revelation to eternally valid truths without any existential encounters between God and man." [21] But his later writings found him continuing to use the term. Apparently he never intended to discard it.

Niebuhr insisted that the poetic and religious imagination of the Bible most readily expresses the basis for the doctrine of man. Myths, imaginative pictures of the world shaped in terms of the powers and feelings of man's interior life, are true, but not true in a scientific sense. Biblical symbols are more convincing than the average prose in the attempt to grasp the ineffable. Biblical myths point to truths that logic cannot adequately encompass. Niebuhr wrote that "the temporal process is like the painter's flat canvas. It is one dimen-

sion upon which two dimensions must be recorded." [22]
Consequently Niebuhr used myth, deceiving for the sake of
truth, to express from the experience of the race and the
individual self what is contemporaneously true for all men
at any given moment.

The advantages that Niebuhr found in myth were that (1)
myth pictures the world as a coherent whole and still retains
a relationship with God, (2) myth allows religion to be
independent of science, and (3) myth eliminates the insuffi-
ciencies of a rationalism that substitutes a "first cause" for
God.

Having shown that the competing current anthropologies
do not do full justice to either man's freedom or finiteness,
Niebuhr turned to the Christian revelation. He said that the
Christian God reveals himself to man in two distinguishable
but inseparable ways. Although he did not use the term in
the traditional sense, he said that the first way that God reveals himself can be called a form of general revelation.
This general, or private, revelation is the universal testimony
of every person's consciousness that he touches a reality
beyond himself and nature. God impinges on every man's
consciousness. A characteristic of this experience is the sense
of "being seen, commanded, judged and known from beyond
ourselves." [23]

Niebuhr pointed out that in its personal-individual form,
revelation contains three elements, two of which are sharply
defined and the third not defined at all.

> The first is a sense of reverence for a majesty and of dependence
> upon an ultimate source of being. The second is a sense of moral
> obligation laid upon one from beyond oneself and of moral un-
> worthiness before a judge. The third, most problematic of the
> elements in religious experience, is the longing for forgiveness. All
> three of these elements become more sharply defined as they gain
> the support of other forms of revelation.[24]

These three elements gain the support of other forms of general revelation in the following order: faith concludes (1)

that the "wholly other" is also the Creator, (2) that the sense of moral unworthiness means that God is Judge, and (3) that the longing for forgiveness after judgment implies the tentative assurance that God is also Redeemer. Although these elements are vague in themselves, they provide a point of contact for special-biblical revelation.

Man's longing for forgiveness, the third testimony of general revelation, requires a further revelation to clarify his common human experience. A special revelation is necessary to know more about this Other at the limits of man's consciousness. Without special interpretation, the general revelation involved in conscience becomes falsified. General revelation presents the problem but offers no solution. The record of this disclosure of a special revelation is found in the biblical account.

In general revelation, man feels a sense of moral obligation and judgment. In the biblical revelation, the counterpart of this is the covenant relation between God and his people and its prophetic interpretation. Within the covenant relationship between God and Israel, Prophetism developed and discerned that the people of Israel were not fulfilling the covenant. Prophetism accused Israel of the besetting sin of pride; Israel identified herself too completely with the divine will, whereas in reality Israel was only a historical instrument. The prophets said that man's sin was his unwillingness to depend upon God to make his life secure. Man brings his own destruction when he exceeds the bounds of creatureliness and seeks to make himself God. Once this prophetic interpretation of history is assumed, history justifies it. Prophetism concludes, in its final answer, that God is related to history only in judgment.

Can God cure as well as punish man's sinful pride? This is the question with which the Messianic promises of the Old Testament are concerned. Messianism rejected the Prophetic pessimism that God is related to history only as a Judge; it concluded instead that God would eventually disclose himself and his relation to history in an act of mercy.

Niebuhr said that this debate between Prophetism and Messianism ended in an impasse. The pessimism of Prophetism showed the optimism of Messianism to be an inadequate answer. Thus the Old Testament concluded certain of the justice of God but uncertain about God's love and mercy. God's ability to fulfill history could finally be revealed only in a Christ. The acceptance of this judgment marked the beginning of a revelation of redemption, the revelation of Christ.[25]

Within the context of special revelation, Niebuhr turned to two distinctive biblical teachings about man, man as creature and image of God, and used these two doctrines to clarify and substantiate his original assumption about man's paradoxical environment of nature and spirit, and to refute the competing anthropologies of modern culture. At the same time Niebuhr felt that these two biblical teachings about man gave significance to his doctrine of man's finiteness and nature on the one hand and man's freedom of spirit on the other.

Niebuhr said that the biblical view of man interprets and relates three aspects of existence in a way that distinguishes it from all other views. (1) The first aspect of the biblical view Niebuhr designated as "creaturehood." (2) The biblical view also "emphasizes the height of self-transcendence in man's spiritual stature in its doctrine of 'image of God.' " (3) The biblical view affirms that the evil in man is a consequence of his inevitable though not necessary unwillingness to "acknowledge his dependence, to accept his finiteness and to admit his insecurity, an unwillingness which involves him in the vicious circle of accentuating the insecurity from which he seeks escape." [26]

The Bible recognizes with humility and reverence, said Niebuhr, that it was a part of God's plan to create man finite, dependent, and mortal. This is true of man's collective and national life as well as his individual life. This creatureliness was pronounced good at the creation. The doctrine of the "resurrection of the body" indicates that man the creature is destined to participate in the fulfillment of life. At the same time, the self has a dynamic existence between nature and spirit. When the self acts, it is involved in a contradiction between these two areas of its life.

The self also has an area above the realm of nature and spirit from which it can survey these two realms. Niebuhr said that Christianity identifies this point of transcendence with the image of God. Christianity understands man primarily from the standpoint of God, and not from the uniqueness of his rational faculties or as a creature of nature. The image of God is the aspect of man's nature which enables him to transcend the world of finitude and see the world from the point of view of eternity. This self-conscious transcendence gives man the ability of self-determination above nature. Man can transcend both nature and himself. This is the freedom side of man's paradoxical nature. The true paradoxical character of man's nature (as image and creature) is indicated in the concrete and earthly choices of man. These choices of the will show that man is both free and determined.

For Niebuhr, Christ revealed the true nature of the self and of God. Christ as the norm for the self points out two characteristics of the self in the image of God. (1) When the transcendent self makes a choice it requires and demands a transcendent norm above itself: this norm is God.[27] (2) The image-of-God doctrine implies that man has a capacity for religious judgments, an ability to judge false gods. Man constantly makes false gods, but by virtue of the image of God he can judge them.[28] This ability to judge false gods does not give man a vision of the true God, but it opens the door for a true revelation. Man's contradictory existence, as free in the image of God and as finite in his creatureliness, presents the "occasion" of sin. This situation of contradiction is not sinful, but it provides the opportunity for sin.

For Niebuhr, the dimension of freedom was the most significant element in human nature; it is the essence of man in the image of God. The freedom of the self raises man above nature and the structure of reason, leading man to the sphere of the spiritual, where he encounters God. In and through freedom man finds a point of contact with God.

The freedom of the self gives life a creative power; but inextricably interwoven into the creative power of freedom is its destructive power. The spiritual freedom of man that increases human values can also be used for their decrease. Man in the image of God does not guarantee his virtue. Man's freedom makes both his destructive and creative powers unique. "Human nature is, in short, a realm of infinite possibilities of good and evil because of the character of human freedom." [29] This tension, as Niebuhr defined it, is a normal aspect of human nature. Any definition of man embraces these two correlatives of freedom.

If the self is to remain a true self, these correlative options of freedom to create or to destroy must attend the self throughout its history. To destroy one would be to destroy the other. Each achievement of good in history will be attended by the possibility of its parallel evil. Niebuhr said that if "biblical thought seems to neglect the creative aspect of the extension of human powers in its prophecies of doom upon proud nations, this is due only to the fact that it is more certain than is Greek thought that, whatever the creative nature of human achievements, there is always a destructive element in human power." [30] These options provided Niebuhr with the foundation for a doctrine of sin on the one hand and a doctrine of growth in grace on the other.

The self, according to Niebuhr, lives in a contradictory environment of nature and spirit. This paradoxical environment includes other subordinate correlatives of finitude and freedom, time and eternity, necessity and freedom, creature and Creator, freedom to create good and to destroy, and other contradictory aspects of human existence. The various philosophies of modern culture fail to take the whole self or its full environment into account. Only the Christian faith does full justice to the self.

The contradictory situation of the self is not evil, but it

leads to the temptation from which evil arises. Man's involvement in finiteness and freedom generates insecurity and
anxiety. Man's insecurity, along with the vision of the unlimited possibilities of creative human freedom, inevitably
tempts man to sin. The biblical interpretation of sin is the
third aspect of the doctrine of man that sharply distinguishes
the Christian view from alternative views. Niebuhr's account
of how sin arises and the various forms it takes is the subject
of chapter 3.

III. Man the Sinner

Niebuhr has been called the twentieth-century theologian of sin. Because of his extensive writing on the subject of sin, the erroneous impression has grown up that Niebuhr was exclusively interested in this one doctrine, that it made him a pessimist, and that he neglected the Christian doctrine of grace. Too many Niebuhr readers have read volume 1 of his Gifford Lectures (the second half of which deals with sin) and have either failed to read or to take seriously volume 2 (which deals with the Christian answer to sin in terms of grace).

Niebuhr's critics have said that he paid an inordinate amount of attention to the doctrine of sin. They have said that it was his controlling insight, the most fundamental of his ideas, the clue to his anthropology, and his most valuable contribution to contemporary theology. Some liberal critics seem to have blamed him for sin because he rediscovered some of its dimensions. My own feeling is that this doctrine was not his central concern, although it was a central pole around which his writings gathered. Sin is the best-known aspect of his work (and has received a disproportionate

amount of discussion), but it is misleading to think that this
doctrine is the launching pad for his thought. I would in
no way minimize the immense significance of his treatment
of sin, but I believe he spoke of it in the light of the shallow
moralism of both theological orthodoxy and liberalism, and
as one part of the task of relating Christianity to the twentieth
century. He is remembered more for his essays on sin than
for his vision of grace. But his impact during the '30s and
'40s was dependent as much upon where his listeners were
as upon what he said. The situation in America called out
for his analysis of the human condition. I hope in the next
chapter to show that he also spoke about God's grace.

There is no question that a numerical count in his written
works would show that he used the word *sin* and its correlatives much more than he did *grace* and its attendant words
of redemption. But when Niebuhr began to write his first
articles and books, the concept of sin had virtually disap-
peared from the vocabulary of enlightened theologians. One
of Niebuhr's early efforts was to reinstate the concept of sin,
to reinterpret it, and to attack moral optimism. In doing
this he "has given us one of the most astute analyses of
the source of sin in human nature which Christian thought
has ever achieved." [1] Niebuhr's thought may be more readily
understood if approached on the avenue of this doctrine, but
it cannot be fully understood if the other aspects are omitted.
Niebuhr said that he attempted to emphasize both man's
Godlikeness and his sin. If the doctrine of sin received a
strong emphasis in his writings, it was because he was attempting to save modern Christianity and culture from the
sentimentality into which it had fallen "by its absurd insistence upon the natural goodness of man." [2] For him there
was no way to understand God's grace without understanding
sin; he pointed to the depths of sin in order to lead to the
heights of grace.

Niebuhr readily admitted that much of his writing and
speaking had been diagnostic; it was so designed to call

modern man to look at his situation. When this was in a partial way being accomplished, Niebuhr advocated a more positive approach and apparently intended to practice it himself. It is ironic that Niebuhr should have been so successful in his analysis of sin that his solution to it has been neglected.

THE ORIGIN OF SIN

Niebuhr named three distinctively Christian affirmations about man that sharply distinguished the Christian from all alternate views. The first two, already considered in the previous chapter, were man as creature and as the image of God. The third affirmation was that man is a sinner. Sin is occasioned, although not caused by, the first two contradictory elements of finiteness and freedom. According to biblical faith, this contradiction does not of necessity betray man into sin.

Niebuhr was more concerned about the nature of sin than its matrix; but an account of its origin also gives a clue to its nature. A bundle of originating factors can be distinguished in Niebuhr's treatment of the emergence of sin. (1) Man is in a unique position between nature and spirit as a free creature. (2) The devil presents to man the temptation to reject the position to which he has been appointed by his Creator. (3) The third element, growing out of the previous two, is man's anxiety to secure his own position in contrast to the original order of God. Once man has rejected his dependence on God, he becomes even more conscious of his insecurity; as a result his anxiety reaches unbounded proportions. These three intertwined aspects of man's initial break from God lead to the manifold forms of sin in the individual and the group. Niebuhr did not distinguish these three factors in the emergence of sin as sharply as this; he thought of them as interdependent and closely related.

Niebuhr saw the self participating in the double environment of nature and spirit with its correlatives of greatness and weakness.[3] In this situation the whole self exhibits capacities for both good and evil. The contradictory character of human existence is not evil in itself. Man's essence resides in his freedom. Sin is not possible without freedom, but it does not necessarily follow from it.[4] The issue in Niebuhr's doctrine of sin is not man's finiteness in nature, but his abortive attempts to escape that finiteness. "Sin in history is not finiteness and particularity," [5] he said. Man's situation of finiteness and freedom is actually a good thing, ordained by God. The situation becomes the locus of sin only when it is falsely interpreted.

If man conscientiously took into account his full involvement in both nature and spirit, he would not be deluded into unwarranted megalomanias. An ultimate mystery surrounds the way in which the human situation becomes a sinful situation. This mystery does not easily fit a scheme of rational intelligibility. The two forms of the mystery are man's responsible freedom, despite the determining factors of creaturely finiteness, "and the greater mystery of the corruption of that freedom and resulting sin and guilt." [6] Man becomes confused and falls into sin when he rejects this state of finiteness and freedom and tries to realize himself without divine authority to define his limits.

The alternatives of right and wrong are not inherent in man's situation of finiteness and freedom. Niebuhr used the symbol of the devil to explain the false interpretation by which man is tempted. This biblical symbol indicates that sin did not originate out of man's own nature. Niebuhr said to "believe that there is a devil is to believe that there is a principle or force of evil antecedent to any evil human action." [7] The devil is a symbol that sin is a mysterious offer, a tempting alternative to God's established order.

The Bible uses the myth of the Fall, said Niebuhr, to indicate the nature of this temptation. The serpent, correctly interpreted by Christian theology as the devil, had previously transcended the proper state set for him by God in an attempt

to usurp the place of God. "Before man fell, the devil fell,"
Niebuhr said.[8] The serpent of the myth created in man a
similar desire to break the limits which God had set for him.
Hence a mysterious force of evil exists prior to man's sin,
and man does not face a vacuum. Niebuhr (in a rather inexact
way) wanted the concept of the devil to act as a symbol of
the mysterious offer presented to man to take the alternative
to God's established order of human existence.

Niebuhr was not a system-builder, and his treatment of
the devil is one indication of the gaps in his thought. Re-
grettably, he was not interested in a universal Fall that involved nature and the cosmos, nor did he have much patience
with those who made ontological speculations. He felt that
ontology (an analysis of the structure and character of being
—being-as-such) depersonalized. There are numerous areas
of his thought that would have profited from a more exact
treatment. He preferred descriptive rather than ontological
terms, but he unconsciously used ontology (ontology cannot
be escaped). Historic symbols and careful delineations of the
nature of ultimate reality are both needed as necessary cor-
rectives one to the other.

Man is in a position between nature and spirit. This situation is not evil in itself; but man's involvement in it makes
him susceptible to the devil's misinterpretation of this situation.[9] Thus the human situation becomes the occasion for
man's temptation along three avenues: (1) Man's natural
limitations and finitude as a part of nature create in him a
sense of insecurity. (2) Man is further insecure because in
his self-transcendence he can anticipate the danger of the
future. Death is the ultimate symbol of this danger. (3)
Through his abilities of self-transcendence, man can envision
infinite possibilities of perfection, and he overestimates his
ability. His very insecurity drives him to the necessity of
overestimating his capacity for attaining perfection, since
this must be accomplished before death claims him as its
victim. These various insecurities cause him anxiety. His

freedom, the basis of his creativity, is also his temptation.
Niebuhr said that since man "is involved in the contingencies
and necessities of the natural process on the one hand, and
since, on the other, he stands outside of them and foresees
their caprices and perils, he is anxious." [10]

Niebuhr said that man, "being both free and bound, both
limited and limitless, is anxious. Anxiety is the inevitable
concomitant of the paradox of freedom and finiteness in
which man is involved." [11] This internal response of the self
is morally neutral. Anxiety is a prerequisite to any meaningful action. The outcome of this anxiety can have either a positive or a negative function. Anxiety does not necessarily imply
a negative function; ideally the tensions of life might be sur-
mounted by faith. There is always the possibility that anxiety
may be purged of sinful self-assertion. Anxiety cannot be
regarded as making sin necessary. Anxiety constitutes a
state of temptation, but out of it can arise either faith or sin.
Anxiety as such is not sin; it is the precondition of sin.

Anxiety is a permanent concomitant of freedom. The destructive and creative aspects of anxiety cannot be separated.
Using an analogy, Niebuhr said that it is the condition of the
sailor climbing the mast "with the abyss of the waves beneath
him and the 'crow's nest' above him. He is anxious about
both the end toward which he strives and the abyss of noth-
ingness into which he may fall." [12] The self senses that the
elements of good and evil are present in any act. Anxiety
over the situation of insecurity does not become operative
as sin until lack of faith enters in. In his ambiguous situation
man feels insecure without a faith in God. Man inevitably
tries to overcome this anxiety by setting up false gods. Under-
neath all the forms of particular sin lies the initial sin of
unbelief—the unwillingness to trust God to keep one secure
amidst the insecurities of existence. This "is the meaning of
Kierkegaard's assertion that sin posits itself," [13] Niebuhr
said. This desire for security is never satisfied; it is indeterminate.

Society, just as the individual self, is faced with the

consequences of anxiety because it too consciously exists in the tension between nature and spirit, necessity and freedom. Nature's necessities must be accepted, but freedom keeps tempting communities with the possibility of escape. The result is an anxious search for security. Just as anxiety can lead the individual self to be creative or destructive, or both at the same time, so it can lead every human group to be creative or destructive. Thus the community is an ethical agent responsible for moral action.

Niebuhr characterized the nature of sin by numerous descriptions which can be placed very generally into two categories. The first is rebellion against God and the order he has established for man's life. This has a religious dimension because it is the attempt to usurp the place of God. Niebuhr used many expressions to describe this rebellion, among them "wrong use of freedom," "rebellion against God," "worship of false centers, eternals, or absolutes," "falling short of the ultimate ideal," "self-worship," and "man's pretension that he is not contingent." [14]

The second category has to do with the human values that the self destroys, either its own or those of others. This has a social dimension because it treats other personalities as if they were of inferior significance. Some of Niebuhr's expressions to describe this second level of sin were "pride," "injustice," "sensuality," "consistent self-interest at the expense of others" (self-centeredness, self-assertion, etc.), "transmuting the will-to-live into the will-to-power," and the "violation of the love obligation between persons." Both categories involve, in varying degrees, a consciously perverse choice of evil. And since man chooses evil, his sin cannot be blamed on his finitude, a defect in his nature, his ignorance, or an evolutionary hangover from his animal ancestry.

THE FORMS OF SIN

When anxiety has conceived within the individual it brings forth both pride and sensuality. Man falls into pride when

he attempts to replace God; he falls into sensuality when he
attempts to escape his freedom. Anxiety is the soil in which
sin grows. Lack of trust in God leads to egotistic self-
assertiveness in individual and collective life (save for the
"second Adam"). This whole process of the centralization of
the ego Niebuhr summed up in the word *pride*. This is man's
basic sin—his unwillingness to acknowledge his creatureliness, his self-elevation.

Niebuhr's analysis of the sin of pride was both profound
and convincing. A careful study of it leaves the reader with
a sense of discomfort about his own pretentiousness. His
treatment imposes upon the reader the task of not allowing
himself to be deceived by the attempts of individuals and
groups to hide their guilt before God by so-called good works.
He further imposes on the reader the task of recognizing
the differences in guilt among men. He convincingly disen-
tangled the various strands of pride and presented them in
ascending sequence, one of the keenest products of his
thought that was to become a "modern classic."

In order to relate this concept of sin to the observable
behavior of men, Niebuhr distinguished among four types of
pride. First was the pride of power. This kind of pride can
rest either upon the self's assumption of its own self-
sufficiency or self-mastery, or upon the self's feeling of
insecurity and the wish to gain self-sufficiency through more
power. In the one case the self does not realize its insecurity;
in the other it is most acutely aware of it. One group in
society lusts for power because its position is secure; another
group, because of its sense of insecurity. In the modern era,
a particularly flagrant form of the will-to-power that tries
to eliminate insecurity is greed.[15] While the man of power
remains something of a beast of prey, those who suffer under
him become vindictive (and thus self-righteous).

Intellectual pride is a sublimation of the pride of power.
All human knowledge pretends to be more true than it is, to
be final and ultimate knowledge. Pride of intellect, like the

pride of power, is derived from either the ignorance of finiteness or the insecurity resulting from the recognition of finiteness. Each great thinker imagines himself the final thinker and thus becomes fair sport for any wayfaring cynic. The thinker cannot imagine that he is subject to the same error that he has detected in others. Intellectual pride is more productive of evil than the simpler will-to-power.

Elements of moral pride are involved in intellectual pride. Intellectual pride claims final truth; implied in this is the claim to absolute morality. Moral pride claims that its standard of righteousness is the final standard; that makes its virtue the vehicle of a pharisaic sin. Niebuhr said that moral pride "is revealed in all 'self-righteous' judgments in which the other is condemned because he fails to conform to the highly arbitrary standards of the self." [16] The self-righteous are guilty of history's greatest cruelties. Most evil is done by good people who do not know that they are not good.

Spiritual pride is an immediate offspring of moral pride. In its quintessential form it is self-glorification. It claims that the self's righteousness conforms to God's righteousness. Niebuhr quoted with approval a comment that most "religion" is unbridled human self-assertion in religious disguise. He said that most religion is merely a "battleground between God and man's self-esteem." [17] There is no final guarantee that man can escape this spiritual pride. Christianity is a religion that can shatter this pride, but the self can become proud of even this shattering experience, and turn its contrition into self-righteousness. Niebuhr approved of Luther's insistence that the vicar of Christ on earth is bound to be the Antichrist.

Dishonesty is related to pride, although not the basis of it. The deception about one's own status is neither pure ignorance nor pure dishonesty. It is partly ignorance because the self inevitably believes itself to be the whole world, and resorts to deception to maintain its security. This is the lie involved in sin. Dishonesty is sin's final expression.

Niebuhr treated the pride of the individual and the group
separately because collective pride is the outgrowth of individual pride; but this collusion of individual egos results in
a unity which transcends the power and pretension of the
individual ego. "The group is more arrogant, hypocritical,
self-centered and more ruthless in the pursuit of its ends than
the individual," [18] he said. Groups have always succumbed to
making idolatrous claims for themselves. Men have further
added to their sin by their unwillingness to recognize this
tendency. Niebuhr's political realism grew out of the conviction that the egoism of the group is stronger than its sense
of justice. Special privileges make all men dishonest.

Collective pride is man's last effort to deny his contin-
gency; it is the very essence of human sin. Collective pride
is a more fruitful source of guilt because it is a more preg-
nant source of injustice. Niebuhr said that the spiritual pride
of nations has two aspects in its unconditional claims: "The
nation claims a more absolute devotion to values which
transcend its life than the facts warrant; and it regards the
values to which it is loyal as more absolute than they really
are." [19] Prophetic religion accurately described this national
self-deification and pronounced judgment upon it. Niebuhr
noted with approval Augustine's having pointed out that such
national pride causes the destruction of every "city of this
world."

Niebuhr gave prolonged attention to the sin of pride—to
the neglect of the other "seven deadly sins." He spent most
of his efforts denouncing the invisible sins of good people,
and seldom wrote about rascals or the visible sins of the
publicly wicked. Niebuhr was certainly aware of the overt
scandals which law enforcers can prevent, but he engaged
himself with the form of evil that laws cannot combat. His
biographer said that he was "less concerned with the three
per cent of American youth who are delinquent than with
the ninety-seven per cent who will grow up to be good citizens." [20] Thus he almost never wrote about what most

Christians denounce as sin. "One hunts long in his writings before finding mention of murder or theft, for example, and when these do appear it is likely to be in their collective, rather than individual form: Nazi murders, or Soviet thefts of neighboring lands." [21]

Niebuhr gave no attention to the sins of indifference. John C. Bennett, his friend, colleague, and affectionate critic, has observed that Niebuhr himself was so incapable of apathy that he could find no place for it in his doctrine. Niebuhr never discussed the traditional sin of sloth. Thus the sin of the weak man who needs some discipline is unaccounted for in his categories. And this is a great loss, because most of us are not in a position to commit the sin of the wise, the powerful, or the good—the sins of the strong who throw their weight around. Niebuhr took the side of those hopelessly buried in the struggle, but defeatism was not one of his characteristic themes.

Niebuhr's treatment of pride was not unique: it had its foundation in Pauline, Augustinian, and Lutheran theology. The importance of his statement of the sin of pride lay in the relevant manner in which he applied it to the many aspects of contemporary life. Few theologians would differ with Niebuhr's structure for the treatment of man's self-love. He encountered considerable opposition, however, about the "inevitable but necessary" character of sin. This will be considered shortly.

Secular thinkers gave Niebuhr's doctrine a different reception. Niebuhr's insistence on the sin of man's self-love met with serious challenges by some of the most astute contemporary minds. Carl R. Rogers, a justly famous modern psychologist, said that Niebuhr's contention that man is primarily the victim of self-love can be maintained only if one views individuals on the most superficial or external basis. Rogers, drawing upon thirty years of psychotherapeutic experience with maladjusted individuals, maintained that the chief difficulty with individuals is that they do not love themselves enough. Individuals despise themselves. Only as the individual senses something lovable in himself, in spite of his mistakes, can he realize himself and love others as he should.

Niebuhr might possibly have answered that Rogers's client undervalued himself because he had a form of pride masquerading as self-deprecation, and it was a temporary condition. Or, Niebuhr might have answered that Rogers's client was sincere, and that self-love had turned into weakness (as will be seen in Niebuhr's treatment of the loss of the self in sensuality). Niebuhr would probably have maintained that self-love and underevaluation are closely related phenomena.

Niebuhr's and Rogers's findings apparently belie one another completely. Both men owe a great debt to Kierkegaard's doctrine of choosing to be a self as the antidote to despair. Anxiety is the precondition to this choice. Self-love is one form that anxiety may drive to in an effort to avoid despair and insecurity. Another escape reaction is to lose oneself in what Niebuhr called sensuality. This has a similarity in Rogers's idea of the self's deprecation of itself. I am not attempting to reconcile the two men, because that is hardly possible; yet I would point to the possibility that Niebuhr may have included Rogers's "lack of self-acceptance" under his doctrine of sensuality, a derivative form of pride and self-love. Or, if he had developed such a doctrine, he might have included it in a doctrine of "sloth." Further, Niebuhr's doctrine of God's grace would find a congenial overlap in Rogers's ideas on "acceptance."

The second general type of sin named by Niebuhr was sensuality. Sensuality, like pride, must be understood in the framework of nature and spirit. While pride attempts to identify the self with spirit, sensuality attempts to identify the self with nature.[22] Sensuality is a more apparent form of anarchy than selfish pride. Niebuhr, calling upon Paul and Augustine, said that sensuality was a fruit of the more primal sin of rebellion against God. Sensuality is not regarded as a natural fruit of man's animal nature. He said that "sensuality is, in effect, the inordinate love for all creaturely and mutable values which result from the primal love of self, rather than love of God." [23]

Niebuhr maintained that sensuality was both a form of idolatry which made the self god, and an alternative idolatry in which the self, conscious of the inadequacy of its self-worship, sought escape by finding some other god.[24] He described three forms of sensuality (luxury, drunkenness, and sexual passion) to demonstrate this. The misuse of things, alcohol, and sex is either an attempt to escape the ego or to enhance the ego; it is either flight or assertion. Sensuality in the individual has its counterpart in society as anarchy (destroying the unity of the group).

Niebuhr summed up the sin of sensuality by pointing out three of its invariable characteristics: a self-defeating self-love, an attempt to escape the self by finding a god outside the self (in a person or process), and an attempt to escape from the confusion caused by sin into some form of subconscious existence. Sensuality begins with self-love or self-gratification. Futility soon ensues, and sensuality becomes self-escape in forms of indulgence that soon reach a point where they defeat their own ends. When a sensuous process is deified it proves disillusioning, and a plunge into unconsciousness is made.[25]

Niebuhr's discussion of sensuality provides us another point of regret in his thought. Although interesting, accurate, and insightful, it lacks the convincing power found in his approach to pride. He treated it as a degraded form of pride, almost as an afterthought. He could have contributed immeasurably to our understanding if he had devoted himself to a full study of sensuality. As it is, contemporary theology usually turns to the findings of depth psychology because it has no formulated doctrine of sensuality of its own.

ORIGINAL SIN AND MAN'S RESPONSIBILITY

Niebuhr said that the forms of actual sin appearing as pride and sensuality derive from a misinterpretation of man's paradoxical position in nature and spirit. Anxiety, which is morally neutral, is antecedent to this misinterpretation. Anxiety presupposes a choice between good and evil. Human experience, however, indicates that man invariably chooses evil. The inevitability of man's choice of evil and his responsibility for having done so, logically irreconcilable facts of experience, formed for Niebuhr the problem of *original sin.* He said:

> Here is the absurdity in a nutshell. Original sin, which is by definition an inherited corruption, or at least an inevitable one, is nevertheless not to be regarded as belonging to his essential nature and therefore is not outside the realm of his responsibility. Sin is natural for man in the sense that it is universal but not in the sense that it is necessary.[26]

Niebuhr believed that both contentions must be maintained, even if they are an offense to rationalists and moralists.

The doctrine of original sin was the crux of Niebuhr's treatment of sin and is probably the one aspect of his thought more than any other that shook American theology loose from its liberal premise. This doctrine also threw him farthest into the American theological thicket. Here he encountered the most difficulty, gave the most paradoxical answer, was open to the most misunderstanding, and emerged with the least satisfying solution. A charming doggerel written by William Temple, Archbishop of Canterbury, after Niebuhr had been lecturing in Swanwick, England, points to this unfortunate misunderstanding. Temple wrote:

> At Swanwick, when Niebuhr had quit it,
> Said a young man: "At last I have hit it.
>   Since I cannot do right,
>   I must find out tonight
> The best sin to commit—and commit it."

This is not to say that Niebuhr may not have been correct in his treatment of original sin; he was dealing with a most difficult subject. Niebuhr had no simple and easy definition of original sin, and he halted before its mystery. Like many men before him, he was not afraid to maintain that all human actions are sinful.

Niebuhr did not follow the traditional interpretation of this doctrine. He saw it no longer as an event in the past, but as a symbolic truth about man's universal and incorrigible tendency to sin. Original sin is centered in human existence. Man does not inherit the guilt of a historical Adam; man falls naturally and inevitably into the sin of claiming eternal worth for his relative objectives. Sin grows out of man's present freedom rather than a prehistoric event of the past.

Niebuhr relied on Sören Kierkegaard to help him unravel the problem of original sin, and he probably cannot be appreciated until this linkage with Kierkegaard is understood. Kierkegaard renewed the doctrine of original sin in an ingenious modern fashion by giving it a "psychological" explanation. Niebuhr accepted this account. To Kierkegaard the ultimate origin of sin was mysterious; but he argued that the psychological conditions under which it took place could be investigated. These conditions involve (1) man's double nature as animal and spirit, (2) the resultant state of unstable anxiety, and (3) the inevitable sprouting of sin. Kierkegaard said that sin was inevitable, but he left room for man's responsibility in succumbing to temptation. Man sins inevitably, but not from natural causality or ontological necessity.

Sin for Kierkegaard was not foreign. Sin cannot be separated from man. Adam is disclosed as a potential sinner by his temptation. The tradition stemming from Kierkegaard says that whenever man becomes self-conscious he has the feeling that he is falling short of what is required of him. "Original sin" is the existential formula to express this condition.

Niebuhr accepted Kierkegaard's analysis and said that, while it may be logically absurd, it is psychologically sound.

When men analyze their own psychological experience of
wrongdoing they must arrive at this conclusion. Existential
experience discloses that man sins inevitably, yet not by
necessity. Man's responsibility shows that he is free, but he
is free only to sin. This is the paradox that Niebuhr called
"original sin."

No doubt it is true that psychological analysis yields such
a verdict as Niebuhr claimed. But it does not give an answer
as to why sin should be inevitable and yet man responsible.
Kierkegaard's speculation that "sin presupposes itself" is
impressive but confusing. (Kierkegaard would probably have
replied that sin is a confusing and mysterious experience.)
Niebuhr said that, when the psychological facts are investigated in their full complexity, it becomes clear that man
sins inevitably, yet without escaping responsibility. The inevitability of sin is not a logical outgrowth of man's situation
in nature and spirit; but temptation to sin lies in this
situation. Ideally, it is possible that anxiety could lead the
self to submit to God's will. It is when anxiety leads the self
to find its life independently, without God, that it falls into
sin and loses its life. The inevitability of sin is "anxiety
plus sin." [27]

When man acts, his action is always evil. Man has the freedom to act, and to contemplate the moral character of his
willful act. In this contemplative examination, the self discovers that a degree of conscious dishonesty was involved in
its sinful act. The self discovers that it was not blindly led to
do evil—that it bears responsibility for its sin. This discovery
is possible because the self can transcend its actions in contemplation. This contemplation involves both the discovery
and the reassertion of freedom.

Sinful actions are followed by remorse or repentance.
To Niebuhr, this attested the fact of responsibility. The self
discovered, both in its act and the contemplation of the act,
that a degree of conscious disharmony accompanied its sinful
act. He said that the "remorse and repentance which are con-

sequent upon such contemplation are similar in their acknowl-
edgement of freedom and responsibility and their implied
assertion of it." [28] Repentance is freedom with faith while
remorse is freedom without faith.

Niebuhr's position was logically absurd. His belief in the
universality of sin stood in contradiction to his belief that
sin was an expression of man's freedom. Niebuhr was not
unique in the way he combined these contradictory elements
into one view; they were left to stand in opposition by Paul,
Augustine, Aquinas, Luther, Calvin, and Pascal. Rationalists
have admired the way that Niebuhr diagnosed the forms of
pride and have even accepted his view about anxiety; but
they have recoiled from this final paradox of original sin.

Niebuhr was well aware of the logical absurdity of this
paradox; still he clung to it as an attempt to bring out a
distinction of which language is not fully capable. He felt
that "loyalty to all the facts may require provisional defiance
of logic." [29] Whether or not the Niebuhr reader will accept
this logical absurdity depends upon his orientation toward
the Pauline tradition. Respected Christian thinkers have held
to a serious doctrine of sin without following the paradoxical
interpretation of existence advocated by Niebuhr. One must
make a choice as to which of the approaches most nearly conforms to the facts of experience as he can best see them.

Niebuhr's statement of the Fall and of original sin does
not stand without opposition. Orthodox theology rejects the
way Niebuhr altered the traditional concept of original sin
from a historical incident to an existential experience. Orthodoxy cannot see that original sin may be true in every moment
of existence but have no history. Even when the doctrine of
original sin has been purged of literalistic errors, Niebuhr's
approach has been rejected by the Pelagian temper that the
free will can attain righteousness. Pelagianism dismisses the
Fall as an unnecessary theological pessimism. Modern liberal
Christianity believes that it can ignore the doctrine of original
sin in its definition and attainment of the good, both indi-

vidually and socially. Practically every school of modern
culture rejects the doctrine of original sin. No evidence to the
contrary presented by realistic theology in the past years
seems to disturb modern man's good opinion of himself.
There are some pessimists among modern secularists, but
they nevertheless have an easy conscience because they do not
hold man responsible for his sin. Even among those who have
lost their easy conscience, there is no disposition to turn to
God for forgiveness and grace; they can "make it on their
own, thank you."

The real question is whether Niebuhr's doctrine of original
sin is an accurate description of existence, and whether or
not Niebuhr's particular interpretation is substantiated by the
facts of contemporary life. For Niebuhr, the psychological
and moral connotations of the Fall were more important than
the ontological ones. He felt that a nonacademic "empiricism"
takes the psychological and moral implications of human
egotism for granted in all forms of human relations. All men
of affairs in business and government act on the basis of an
implied doctrine of original sin. Niebuhr said that the "wisdom of the 'man in the street' never fails to comprehend the
mixture of creativity and self-concern in the behavior of all
his fellows." [30] This implied recognition of the harsh reality
of original sin on the part of the nonacademic man does not
imply, however, that Niebuhr's particular approach was a
correct one. On the other hand, it does mean that Niebuhr the
analyst and the existential man recognized that all of the
facts involve a dialectical statement of the self's inevitable
self-assertion and its consequent responsibility.

ORIGINAL RIGHTEOUSNESS

Niebuhr held that no man is able to regard his sin as
normal, regardless of how deeply involved in it he is. There
lingers in man's soul a memory of a condition of blessedness,
a sense of an original righteousness that is no longer his

possession. This sense of a contradiction between what man is and what he ought to be is a universal experience.

Niebuhr said that Christian thought had confused the relation of man's original righteousness to his sinful nature in history by assigning the original righteousness to a paradisiacal period before the Fall of Adam. Original righteousness is a vertical relation, and when "the Fall is made an event in history rather than a symbol of an aspect of every historical moment in the life of man, the relation of evil to goodness in that moment is obscured," he said.[31]

Faith, hope, and love were the virtues designated by Niebuhr as filling the content of original righteousness. They are the basic requirements of freedom, exhausting the definition of original righteousness. There is no point of advance beyond them. Faith gives harmony toward God. Hope, a form of faith, is harmony within the self. Love, a derivative of faith, is harmony toward others that allows for living in community. These three virtues can be reduced to the one virtue of the self's perfect relationship to God. Faith, hope, and love are the source of original righteousness; their fulfillment *is* original righteousness. They are not static terms, but dynamic expressions of man's activity. The virtues of faith, hope, and love appear to sinful man in the form of law. In fact, these virtues heighten the sense of sin. They either show that man falls short of them, or they tempt man to assume that he can live up to them because he knows them. This law is written in man's heart, and his conscience constantly reminds him of it.

Niebuhr said that when man examines his conduct in the light of original righteousness he discovers that, while he gives assent to it in the transcendent self, he never lives up to it in his acting self. Man finds he has fallen. The fall happens in that moment of freedom when the free self, agreeing with the law of agape, looks down into the empirical self and discovers selfishness. Psychologically, every man is his own Adam.

The question naturally arises, What is the possibility of

fulfilling original righteousness for the acting and sinful self? Niebuhr said that the perfect harmony toward God that eliminates anxiety is not a simple possibility of human existence; this freedom from anxiety belongs to the perfection before the Fall. The will cannot do the good that it wishes. Even in acts of obedience to God there is an inner contradiction. Original righteousness becomes a demanding law to the sinful man. Original righteousness is only a possibility, and never a possession of the self in action. Niebuhr's critics usually draw the conclusion from this statement that he was an utter pessimist.

The salient features of Niebuhr's doctrine of sin, then, are the universality of sin, sin's existence as an objective fact in human experience, sin's tendency to perpetuate and aggravate itself, a meaningful sense in which there is bondage of the will, and the inability of man to extricate himself from the situation of unbelief. Yet Niebuhr maintains that man has a real responsibility for his self-assertion and lack of trust in God. Further, Niebuhr provides a rationale for good works, though not in the sense of bargaining merits with God.

Niebuhr said that pre-Reformation Christianity taught that man under grace (defined primarily as power) could realize original righteousness. This idea was taught, however, with restrictions and reservations. The Reformation, defining grace primarily as forgiveness, taught that not even the redeemed man could overcome his contradiction and embody original righteousness. The Renaissance, the other wing that came out of the breakup of the medieval synthesis, saw human nature only as a realm of limitless possibilities. According to Niebuhr, both modern liberal Christianity and secular culture adopted the Renaissance answer to man's attainment of original righteousness. He proposed to take what was valid in the insights of both Renaissance and Reformation and combine them into a more fruitful approach. He intended his answer to have all the benefits of grace as both power and forgiveness.

IV. The Triumph of Grace

If Niebuhr's doctrine of sin is the best known but most misunderstood of his teachings, then his doctrine of grace is the least known and least appreciated of his teachings. His doctrine of grace—God's power *over* man and *in* man—is practically an unrecognized element in his theology. Since the doctrine of sin is the only element known by some of his critics, a common conclusion is that Niebuhr was too pessimistic about human nature, that he saw only man's sin, and that he offered no proximate or ultimate hope. Conventional wisdom says that Niebuhr photographed the problem of evil and displayed the photograph in the public art gallery, that he made his strongest appeal to the pessimists, and that his faith in sin left him devoid of a program of redemption. Don't believe these rumors; they are misleading. He was vastly more hopeful than many of his critics realize.

A smaller group of more sympathetic critics recognize that Niebuhr had a doctrine of grace, but they feel that it was less than adequate. Some of them say that his doctrine was practically extinguished by his pessimism, that Niebuhr was more a John the Baptist than a St. John. Some defend him by saying that he was not a prophet of gloom, and that

he had a healthy doctrine of redemption. But these Niebuhr
sympathizers have contented themselves with mentioning his
doctrine of grace without demonstrating it. A third group
says that Niebuhr's doctrine of grace is wholly eschatological
and not immediately redemptive. In general, then, his doctrine of grace has been denied, distorted, or neglected by his
critics, both friendly and unfriendly.

For such treatment Niebuhr was partly to blame, and
these misunderstandings have just enough truth in them to be
taken seriously. There are several reasons for this continuing
skeptical attitude. (1) The early writings of Niebuhr were
far more concerned with an analysis of man's sins than they
were about God's grace. His early concern was to shatter the
idols of man's self-esteem. The "growth in grace" in his books
came later, finding systematic treatment in volume 2 of his
Gifford Lectures. But his treatment of sin in volume 1 was
lauded and criticized so extravagantly that it overshadowed
the second volume when it appeared two years later. (2)
Niebuhr so insistently warned that even the life of grace is
prone to corruption that his readers gained the impression
that grace is inevitably corrupted by self-righteousness. His
terminology easily gave the impression that the grace of
Christ can win no victories in history. He said that sin is
overcome "in principle" but not "in fact." The apparent implication was that grace is of little aid to man's struggles.
Niebuhr did not so limit the Cross, and he eventually re-
pudiated this confusing terminology as inadequate to "describe the real sanctification that takes place in conversion
when the soul turns from itself to God." [1] (3) A third cause
for skepticism about Niebuhr's doctrine of grace was the
failure to read Niebuhr's occasional writings. His magazine
articles are certainly not as important as his books, but his
books made up only a portion of his writings. In over a
thousand occasional writings he applied his doctrine of grace
to concrete issues, and here it can be seen that his theology
did not result in moral paralysis.

Niebuhr's doctrine of grace was as central and essential

to his theology as his doctrine of sin or any other doctrine. Niebuhr had a great deal to say about man's condition in sin; but he also spoke with assurance about God's answer to man's sin. To be sure, Niebuhr set his doctrine of grace against a dark background of original sin. He said that the "Christian doctrine of grace stands in juxtaposition to the Christian doctrine of original sin and has meaning only if the latter is an accurate description of the actual facts of human experience." [2] He painted a dark picture of man's sin in order to show his need for grace. He said it "is from the diagnosis of impotence that the doctrine of grace achieves its significance; for grace is the answer to the human problem. Grace is consistently both power and pardon." [3] He felt that liberal Christians and secularists had disregarded the Christian experience of grace because of their ignorance about sin.

Niebuhr affirmed that the Christian doctrine of salvation by grace was the only cure for original sin. He said we "assert as Christians that the message of Christ is a source of grace and truth to all men either in their individual dimensions or in the social dimension of their existence." [4] The major problems of living cannot be solved without salvation by grace. Further, the "facts of history and these Scriptural injunctions must warn us that it is the business of the Christian church to bear witness . . . to the grace of Christ which saves all who truly repent of their sins." [5]

In one sense, then, Niebuhr's appraisal of the human situation was negative. But there was a divine grace greater than either man's sin or righteousness to which he ultimately turned. An educated optimism shines out in his later writings. He can be considered to hold a balance of pessimism and optimism, retaining the values of each and avoiding the errors he saw in both.

THE IMPORTANCE OF CHRIST

God's grace as Truth and Power come in Christ. Niebuhr's analysis of man's sinful condition showed that the self is

unable to know the truth with its reason and unable to obey
the truth in its will. To relieve the self's reason and will from
this involvement in sin God's grace provides two essential
elements: truth as a norm and power to fulfill the norm.
In Christ the Truth (Son of God and second Adam—
Incarnation-Atonement and sacrificial love) God's grace has
provided the self's norm. In Christ the Power of God (Justification, Sanctification, and eschatological grace) God's grace
gives strength to fulfill the self's life.

Niebuhr did not give a systematic elaboration of his ideas
on Christology. By his own admission, however, Christology
became the center of his thought.

> The situation is that I have come gradually to realize that it is
> possible to look at the human situation without illusion and with-
> out despair only from the standpoint of the Christ-revelation. It
> has come to be more and more the ultimate truth. . . . I have come
> to know with Pascal that only in "simplicity of the Gospel" is it
> possible to measure the full "dignity" and "misery" of man. Thus
> the Christological center of my thought has become more explicit
> and more important. But . . . I have never pretended to be a
> theologian, and so I have elaborated the Christological theme only
> in the context of inquiries about human nature and human history.[6]

In a first reading of Niebuhr's works it is not obvious that
Christology is the leitmotif of his theology; but when his
works are read with this admitted key, they show an intrinsic
unity. Although he was late in emphasizing Christology, he
once remarked that his theology was nothing more than an
analysis of the truth about "Christ for us" in its significance
for man.[7]

Christology has to do with the person and work of Christ.
The Incarnation (God's assumption of human nature and
flesh) and Atonement (the meaning of the death of Jesus)
are the two traditional doctrines for expressing this faith.
Orthodox Christianity has customarily moved from an account of Christ's person (fully divine, fully human) to his

work (revealer of the Father and reconciler to the Father). Niebuhr's early emphasis was upon the transforming power of Christ in the individual and society ("Christ in us"), but his later emphasis shifted to the transcendent reality and truth of Christ ("Christ for us"). His early works showed a liberalism in an unblushing form. This early concern, though liberal, was about the relation of the transforming power of the Cross to the world. The direction of Niebuhr's analysis, like that of the Protestant Reformers, was to show the benefits of Christ. "It is not too much to say that Niebuhr's concern for the relevance of the Christian faith is a twentieth century version of the Reformers' insistence upon 'the benefits of Christ' as the point of departure for a vital and meaningful Christian faith," [8] Paul Lehmann states. The Reformation moved from the benefits of Christ to his promises, from what Christ does to us to what he is for us. Niebuhr followed this tradition.

Niebuhr eventually came to the place in his Christology where he emphasized equally well the truth of the Christian faith and the relevance of this truth to the human situation. The transcendent Christ and the empowering Christ were linked together. The problem came to be how to show that the Cross expressed the transcendent reality of Christ and his transforming power in human nature. This was the central concern of *The Nature and Destiny of Man* and *Faith and History*. The first answer to the sinful human situation was God's grace expressed in Christ as the Truth (Son of God and second Adam).

GRACE AS TRUTH

In the previous chapter we saw that Niebuhr asserted that the self is inevitably involved in evil, both in its reason and its will. The self's reason becomes sinful when it absolutizes a partial perspective. The self in its moments of self-transcendence perverts its limited truths into false absolutes.

The self's will becomes sinful when it confirms the partial perspective of the reason. The concrete action of the human will is invariably sinful. The result is a false truth or norm about which the reason and the will agree. This involves a twofold consequence: the sinful self (1) does not know the truth with its reason and (2) cannot act to obey the truth in its will. According to Niebuhr, God's grace must provide two essential elements in its answer: (1) man must again be provided with the truth as a norm; (2) his will must be freed and provided with the power to obey the truth. Man needs both the truth and the power to fulfill the truth.

In Christ the sinful self finds a truth and norm that transcends its partial perspectives. The will aspect of the human predicament is answered by God's grace in Christ as the power of God (to be treated in the next section of this chapter). This power overcomes man's perverted and impotent will. God's grace in Christ as Truth and Power is inseparable. Niebuhr said that Truth and Power can be separated for the sake of analysis, but they confront the believer in Christ at the same chronological moment. For the sake of analysis, Niebuhr first discussed Christ as Truth. (His two favorite expressions for the norm in Christ were Wisdom and Truth, but for consistency only the expression Christ as Truth will be used in this section.)

The first aspect of the disclosure of Christ the Truth was treated by Niebuhr under the heading of the "Son of God." By that expression Niebuhr meant the Incarnation and the Atonement. The Incarnation clarifies God's relationship to history; the Atonement shows that God has resources of mercy beyond his judgment. "Son of God" is the orthodox way of saying that the Incarnation has really taken place. The Incarnation becomes meaningful, said Niebuhr, when it is understood in relation to the Atonement. The Incarnation is the presupposition of the Atonement, and the Atonement is the distinctive content of the Incarnation. (The second aspect of Christ the Truth was treated by Niebuhr under the heading of "the second Adam"—a disclosure of sacrificial love as the perfect form for human nature.)

The initial step in man's redemption from sin is the recovery of Christ as the Truth. This is a matter of an adequate apprehension of the revelation of Christ. Niebuhr intimately conjoined an analysis of the human situation with revelation to arrive at his doctrine of man. Revelation, according to Niebuhr, was both general (personal-individual) and special (biblical). Each type of revelation is dependent upon the other. Biblical revelation culminates in the Christ who reveals the essential nature of man. This is the Incarnation, the distinctive content of which is the act of Atonement. Hebrew Prophetism and Messianism, unlike nonhistorical religions and cultures, form the preparatory background for the Christ and set the stage for man's restoration.

The Hebrew anticipation of a Messiah laid the foundation for hope of an Incarnation, a Christ. To the Hebrews, history was potentially meaningful because the disclosure of a Christ was expected. The Hebrews expected a Christ because they considered it both possible (history is more than nature-necessity) and necessary (history is fragmentary). A Christ is expected only when man becomes personally aware that he has problems that he cannot solve. Man looks for a Christ only after he understands the full height of his freedom and his full involvement in sin. When man does not know his sin he has no need of God. Niebuhr said that the "sinner who justifies himself does not know God as judge and does not need God as Saviour." [9] An awareness of sin is a first step in the expectation of a Christ; thus Niebuhr felt justified in emphasizing sin first. Divine mercy cannot be experienced until the seriousness of sin is fully known. Only the despair that results from a knowledge that sin causes suffering to God can appropriate divine forgiveness.

To be appreciated a Christ must be expected. Christ was a "stumbling block" to the Jews because he was not the type of Christ they expected, but he was not "foolishness" as he

was to the Greeks.[10] The true Christ can never be the expected
Messiah because Messianic expectations always contain the
egoistic elements of a local culture.

Niebuhr said that the Old Testament prophets finally concluded that God is related to history only in judgment. On
the other hand, the Messianic expectations of the Old Testament realized that man did not fulfill God's will, yet they did
not accept the prophetic conclusion. Messianism felt that the
ideal could be realized in as well as beyond history. It expected God's will to be disclosed and fulfilled at some point
in history. Niebuhr said that Jesus made the prophetic problem the basis of his reinterpretation of Jewish Messianism.
Jesus took over the prophetic insight that Israel was sinful; he
converted it into the insight that only he who acknowledges
his sin is without sin. Niebuhr said that in Jesus' parable of
the Last Judgment, Jesus shows that the distinction between
good and evil is not destroyed; yet in the final judgment, there
are no righteous in contrast to God. This raised the further
problem of how God both condemns man's moral efforts and
yet, in his mercy, recognizes and completes them. This, said
Niebuhr, is answered in Jesus' conception of the suffering
Messiah, the heart of the Atonement.

The "suffering Messiah" shows God's mercy toward man's
incomplete moral efforts as well as his justice in condemning
them. He clarifies the answer to the prophetic problem in a
resource of mercy beyond his judgment which becomes effective as he takes the consequences of his judgment into
himself. The central truth embodied in the doctrine of the
Atonement is that the justice and mercy of God are one.
Niebuhr's chief concern in volume 2 of his Gifford Lectures
was with the truth and relevance of this doctrine.

The Atonement, by relating justice and mercy, wrath and
forgiveness, is a double-dimensional event. The mercy dimension of the Atonement shows God redeeming and com-
pleting the ethical fragmentariness of man. This contradiction
remains in history, while it is resolved on the divine level.

Faith brings a unity into this paradox. Niebuhr said that when man in an attitude of contrition and faith appropriates the divine mercy, the human situation is both understood and overcome. God's power becomes available to man to complete his incompleteness and purge him of his vain efforts at self-completion. When Christ the Truth comes into history he completes incomplete knowledge, clarifies obscurities of history, and corrects man's self-centered interpretation of human existence. In this sense he is a contradiction to human culture, but true wisdom to the man of faith. To the man of faith the revelation of Truth will also become a revelation of Power.

Niebuhr said that the Christian faith accepts the expected Messiah who was rejected by the Jews. St. Paul summarizes the significance the Christian community attributed to Christ by calling him the Power and Wisdom of God (1 Cor. 1:23–24). St. John calls him the Grace and Truth of God (John 1:17). Niebuhr, borrowing this biblical terminology to express the categories of his own Christology, said that Christ the Truth has fully disclosed God's will and purpose for life and history. Christ as Power is God's dynamic authority revealed in such a way that there can be no question of any other power being able to overcome it. Christ is the ultimate expression of God's grace.

According to Niebuhr, then, the Christian faith asserts that the crucified Christ is both Truth and Power. The true norm of life has been revealed along with the power to complete and fulfill it. Power can be mediated to the individual if the truth of the Atonement is appropriated inwardly by faith. Thus "the alternate moods of despair and false hope are overcome and the individual is actually freed to live a life of serenity and creativity." [11]

According to Niebuhr, man is unable to rise above his partial perspectives to grasp the true standards of God, to find his true norm. This condition is answered by the revelation of Christ as the Truth of God. The other facet of the human predicament is that the will of man inevitably corrupts itself in competing interests. The answer to this problem is found in the revelation of Christ as the Power of God.

Before the subject of Christ as Power is considered the second aspect of Christ the Truth (second Adam) must be evaluated. Christ as the second Adam discloses the content of God's grace as Truth that sets man his true norm in history, just as the "Son of God" expresses that the Incarnation and Atonement have taken place.

The point of contact between man and God is love. Man is evil but he knows how to love. The essence of both human nature and God's nature is love. The significance of Christ as the second Adam is the revelation of the true character of both the human and the divine nature. Christ is the norm for human conduct, and its end. Christ has demonstrated the full meaning of what it means to be a man; therefore, he is fully the second Adam, the standard by which God will finally judge man at the end of history. Because of man's freedom, he has some idea of the perfect love of Christ as the norm, though he has never attained it in his own life. Christ, as normative man, belongs to both natural and revealed religion.

As the Son of God, Jesus reveals the divine love that resolves the predicament of history. As the second Adam, he forms the pattern of human perfection. The one love has a divine counterpart, the other a human counterpart. Sacrificial love is the love of the Cross, the perfect love. The Cross is a symbol of man's perfection; and this, rather than a traditional doctrine such as the virgin birth, answered the problem of the sinlessness of Christ for Niebuhr.

It is the conviction of the Christian faith that the agape of Christ is the disclosure of the divine love. Christ is also the disclosure of perfect human love, an "impossible possibility" for man. The love of Christ sets the principles for the Christian interpretation of history. This can be seen when love of the second Adam is related to the first Adam, to mutual love, and to the end of history. Niebuhr analyzed

man's highest possibilities by showing the relation of the
second Adam to the first Adam (man's ultimate and original
perfection), mutual love (the possibilities and limits of
history), and the end of history (how the historical character of the perfection of history is preserved against attempts
to surrender history to eternity in interpreting its fulfillment).

Christ, the perfect norm of human character, reestablishes
the virtue which Adam had before the Fall. The perfection
before the Fall cannot be understood except as it is found in
the perfection of Christ. Once this is understood, it is also
seen that Christ exceeds as well as reestablishes the primitive
perfection.[12]

Mutual love is the first level below sacrificial love. This
love makes social existence possible. This is a lesser form of
love because it is tainted with self-interest. Mutual love,
because of this self-interest, always remains partly a contradiction of sacrificial love. The sacrificial love of Christ
transcends mutual love in a threefold way. Sacrificial love
completes the incompleteness of mutual love, clarifies and defines the ethical possibilities of history, and represents a perfection which contradicts the false pretensions of virtue in
history.[13]

The principle of justice is immediately below the principle
of mutual love. The principle of justice gives support to the
individual's obligation to mutual love. This is a threefold
relation. Principles of justice show that the individual is
obligated to give mutual love in his immediate obligations
to his neighbor on the personal level, in complicated social
interrelations, and in the wider community.

The doctrine of the second Adam, said Niebuhr, refutes
the mystics who seek perfection by a final incorporation into
eternity. The tendency of the mystics is to make gnosis
(knowledge) rather than agape the final form.

The God whom Christians worship reveals his majesty and holiness not in eternal disinterestedness but in suffering love. And the

moral perfection, which the New Testament regards as normative, transcends history not as thought transcends action but as suffering love transcends mutual love. It is an act rather than a thought which sets the Christ above history, and being an act, it is more indubitably in history than a mere thought.[14]

Sacrificial love is ethically normative for the Christian life. Man's highest norm is not a flight from historical vitalities, but a harmony of love which relates itself to others and to God. Although sacrificial love transcends the realities of history (since it is grounded in the character of God), it is nevertheless validated in history where concern for others is manifest. Thus Niebuhr attempted to make the norm of Christ relevant both to man's contemporary situation and his situation at the end of history.

GRACE AS POWER

Niebuhr said that "grace as Power" was the solution to the second aspect of man's sinful situation. Man's will must be freed and provided with the power to obey the truth and live up to the norm expressed in Christ. Man must have God's grace as Power to fulfill his life. It is self-evident that sinful man needs an outside source of power to begin to measure up to his true norm, else he will surrender to despair. Man must be assured of help to sustain interest in this effort.

God's grace is an adequate answer. Christ is the Power as well as the Truth of God. When man confesses his need and helplessness to God, grace as Power is made available for him. God begins by being man's judge, but ends by providing a moral undergirding that empowers history. The self is shattered and forgiven when it confronts Christ as Truth. But at the same time God's grace as Power is imparted to the believer to renew his life and overcome his sin.

Niebuhr differentiated between two facets of grace as Power. The Power of God *over* man is justifying grace that completes what man cannot complete and imputes to him righteousness and forgiveness. The Power of God *in* man is sanctifying grace that provides resources to enable man to become what he truly ought to be. Justification supplies man with a new nature, clears him from God's judgment, and releases him to a life of holiness. Sanctification (synonymous with the gift of the Holy Spirit) empowers the new man with the grace to reach levels of agape that would be impossible under his own power.[15]

Niebuhr said that this analysis of the Power of grace as pardoning and empowering will not convince modern man of its relevance to his situation. Modern man is bent on increasing the power and range of his mind against the narrower impulses of his body. To establish the relevance of the doctrine of grace as Power, Niebuhr applied it to the facts of human experience. In order to show the full implications of the Power of grace as mercy towards (Justification) and power in (Sanctification) man, Niebuhr used the device of an existential explication of Galatians 2:20.

"I am crucified with Christ." Niebuhr used this phrase to describe the initial work of grace that shatters the sinful self into despair and repentance (conversion). This phrase must be taken poetically (and Niebuhr's explication was poetic) because it does not literally mean the destruction of the self. Niebuhr said that Paul's first assertion is that the self which is centered in itself must be "crucified," shattered, and destroyed. This is necessary because of the human situation, already described by Niebuhr in terms of the doctrine of original sin.[16]

"Nevertheless I live." Justification, the assurance of divine mercy and forgiveness, is the immediate consequence of conversion. It is an inner feeling that the ego which has been shattered is now cleansed and forgiven. The Christ who is apprehended by faith imputes his righteousness to the penitent self. The self feels a consequent release and sense of peace. God accepts the self's intention to live by the norm of agape as the *act* itself. The possession of righteousness is

a possession by faith, not by one's own merit. The sense of
peace comes, not because one deserves it, but because the
righteousness of Christ is imputed to the person. Nor is man
constituted perfect through this infused righteousness. The
sinful nature remains, although the self feels at peace with
God. This reconstructed self is a consequence of the invasion
of the Holy Spirit from without.[17]

"Yet not I; but Christ lives in me." Justification releases
the self to an active working out of its own salvation, for it is
God who works both to will and to do. The new self is not
complete with justification. Sanctification is God's empowering of the new self for the performance of agape—an existential moment on the level of moral experience. On this
level also the self's identity is preserved and its new life is
dependent upon a divine source of power, a "power not its
own." But this new life of the self is, in a sense, not fully
complete. This gives a double meaning to the life of the new
self on this last level of regeneration.

Niebuhr said that there is an ambiguity about the relation
of the self to Christ which can be expressed in terms of the
previously mentioned grace as Power over man and Power
in man. The "yet not I" is a confession of the converted self
that its new life is the result of a divinely infused power. The
"yet not I" is also a confession of the converted self that the
new self is not an accomplished reality; "that in every historic concretion there is an element of sinful self-realization,
or premature completion of the self with itself at the centre;
that, therefore, the new self is the Christ of intention rather
than an actual achievement."[18]

Niebuhr maintained that the new life, a product of the
grace of God, is a reality; but the new life is never a fully
accomplished reality. It is fully accomplished in intention
rather than in achievement. Grace does not completely re-
move the contradiction between man and God. Sanctification
is not a thing completed immediately after conversion.

Whenever the sinful self faces up to its self-love in an

attitude of repentance and faith, the consequent experience of release from self creates a concomitant sense of gratitude. The self recognizes that its rebirth is a miracle that it could not have accomplished in its own power. This recognition of the otherness of divine determinism and human responsibility raises the problem of the delicate balance between divine determinism and human responsibility. Niebuhr both asserted and denied the sovereignty of grace. Grace is prior to man's will; but man's cooperation is needed for grace to be effective.

Niebuhr interpreted God's electing grace and man's free will as an existential relation. He said that the relation cannot be subjected to a precise logical analysis. Free will as a force working independently of grace is true on one level of experience, while God's grace as the exclusive source of human redemption is true on another level. Man's freedom to respond to the good is valid on the level of the sinful self. Grace as the power of God to elect man is valid on the level of faith where the self transcends itself. Niebuhr again broke the rules of formal logic to stress an aspect of the self's experience.

Although Niebuhr had reservations about complete sanctification, he gave ample indication that the converted man lives an altogether different quality of life. The traits of the new self are repentant humility (admissions of the self that it falls short of the norm of Christ), faith that God's good will triumph over evils in history, and the characteristic fruits of the Spirit—love, joy, and peace.

Niebuhr's explication of Galatians 2:20 assumed that God's grace as Power for man's life has a double connotation; the first suggests that the new life has been achieved through grace as a power not our own, while the second suggests that the new life is not yet an achieved fact. This second connotation, a qualification of sanctifying grace, Niebuhr said, is also supported by the thought of St. Paul when his thought is considered as a whole. Furthermore, Niebuhr be-

lieved that experience validates the second meaning as well
as the first.

It is difficult to express these two aspects of grace as Power
without unduly emphasizing one side at the expense of the
other. Niebuhr maintained, however, that these two sides of
grace do not contradict but support one another. Niebuhr's
conclusion was that the facts of experience indicate that grace
as justification (forgiveness) and grace as sanctification (en-
duement with power) are both true. On one level the self
experiences renewal and on another level the self remains
guilty. This was designated by Niebuhr as "the paradox of
grace."

THE PARADOX OF GRACE

Niebuhr relied on St. Paul to arrive at his concept of grace
as Power in and over man (*the* central dogma of the Christian faith). He believed that Paul's interpretation of grace
as justification and sanctification were "closely related to
Jesus' insistence that the righteous are not righteous before
the divine judgment; and to his conception of the suffering
Messiah as a revelation of the justice and mercy of God." [19]
At the same time Niebuhr arrived at his "paradox of grace"
by an analysis of its various interpretations through Christian
history. He said that Christians have repeatedly resisted the
paradox and have sought new ways of vindicating men who
have become righteous through Christ. As Niebuhr described
it, the favorite strategy of avoiding the paradox is to claim
the achievement of perfection (which in turn becomes a
source of human arrogance).

Niebuhr evaluated the traditions that accept the concept of
grace as Power. He judged these traditions on the basis of
their retention (or lack of retention) of the delicate balance
between grace as sanctification and as justification. They become a foil for his own interpretation because he found that
each destroyed the paradox. Niebuhr felt that an apprecia-

tion of the paradox of grace can be gained after seeing the easy way it is broken by those who make professions of agape. From an examination of these misinterpretations he drew a synthesis that he felt did justice to the paradox.

Niebuhr said that in the Roman Catholic tradition grace as justification (grace over man) is increasingly subordinated to grace as sanctification (grace in man). This is due to the Roman interpretation of sin "as the privation of an original perfection, rather than as a positive corruption." [20] Grace ceases to be a justifying power and becomes an addition to human nature. Augustine emphasized justification, but he did not fully recognize the "persistent power of self-love in the new life." Later traditions abandoned Augustine's restrictions and identified the Church with the Kingdom of God, which culminated in the distortion of papal infallibility. According to Niebuhr, Rome cannot solve the problem of sin because it will not admit its own proud pretensions.

Niebuhr said that the Roman Church broke the paradox of grace by raising a human institution to an unchallenged position above judgment. The significance of the Protestant Reformation was that it challenged this "curious compound of human self-confidence and gospel humility." The free self cannot honestly deceive itself that it has attained perfect sanctification. This made a challenge inevitable. The Reformation understood (1) that life must be completed by a power that is not our own, (2) that human pride insinuates itself on every level of sainthood, and (3) that freedom can bring either good or evil or both.

The medieval synthesis of humility and self-confidence was challenged by the Renaissance. For Niebuhr the Renaissance was the impulse towards the fulfillment of life in history and included numerous movements from the fourteenth century to the present. The Renaissance combined the classic trust in reason with the Catholic line of perfectionism. The extension of the powers of the human mind became the supposed key to the overcoming of human problems. Grace as a requisite for fulfilling life was dispensed with. Sanctificationist in principle, it brushed aside the idea of justification. The Renaissance went even further, and dismissed the whole idea of grace.

The Renaissance disregarded grace in its concept of the fulfillment of life, and it assumed that all progress meant the advancement of good. The end of history contained only fulfillment. The most grievous error of the Renaissance, according to Niebuhr, was its too-simple conception of historical progress. It was right in conceiving history dynamically; but it conceived the dynamic aspects of history too simply. It did not recognize that history is filled with endless possibilities of both good and evil.

Niebuhr grouped sectarian Protestantism with the Renaissance because it shared the Renaissance emphasis upon grace as Power in man, the impulse toward the completion of life. Niebuhr said that the sects did not understand the limits of personal sanctification. Unlike the Renaissance, however, the sects defined grace "in" man in Christian terms. The sects emphasized sanctification at the expense of justification. This grace could be immediately acquired, and it was accompanied by a specific change in one's manner of life.

There were two impulses in sectarianism: "(a) the impulse towards the perfection of individual life expressed in the pietistic sects and (b) the impulse towards the fulfillment of history expressed particularly in the Anabaptist and socially radical sects." [21] The perfectionist groups (pietistic-mystical) identified the "inner light" with the immanent Christ and exempted the "light" from judgment. The eschatological sects suffered from the coming Kingdom (Anabaptist) or fought for it (Cromwellians), but anticipated it in history.

According to Niebuhr, the Reformation rediscovered the biblical-prophetic insight that sin persists in life and history. The Reformation was the place where "that side of the gospel, which negates and contradicts historical achievements, became more fully known." [22] The Reformation was most fully

aware of the persistence of sin in the life of the saints. The
final completion of life was found in the divine mercy. Only
after history had shown the error of simpler interpretation
was this side of the gospel fully known. This rediscovered
"justification by faith" was frequently given a one-sided emphasis because of the polemical nature of the Reformation.
The Reformation looked for a completion of life from a
power that was not man's own. It denied the implication of
the Catholic theory of grace that life can be brought to a full
degree of completion. It interpreted grace primarily as the
forgiveness of God toward man rather than power in man.
The Reformation most fully comprehended what the Renaissance neglected, the tragic aspect of history. The Reformation, on the other hand, failed to understand the cultural
potentialities of grace.

Niebuhr concluded that neither the insights of Luther nor
Calvin were able to do justice to the paradox of grace or the
problems of the human predicament. Calvinism, like Roman
Catholicism, stressed sanctification to the point that certain
facts of history were beyond judgment and forgiveness.
Lutheranism canceled out the urgency of sanctification by
giving the experience of justification the principal place in
grace. Niebuhr concluded that while "the Lutheran side of
the Reformation always walks on the edge of the precipice
of superamoralism, not to say antinomianism, the Calvinistic
Reformation is imperiled by the opposite danger of a new
moralism and legalism." [23]

Niebuhr said that the spiritual life of recent centuries has
been determined by the interaction between the Renaissance
and the Reformation approaches to existence. They generated
two contrasting types of spirituality, and that "contrast may
well be defined in terms of the 'sanctification' and 'justification' aspects of the Christian doctrine of grace," he said.[24]
The Reformation was overbalanced by a defeatism and cultural obscurantism, and the Renaissance by an unwarranted
optimism.

Niebuhr proposed a new synthesis that fitted together the
two contrasting discoveries of the Renaissance and the Reformation and corrected the one-sided blindness of both. He
stated that this attempt at synthesis was a central problem of
his theology. Niebuhr felt that if he could bring about this
synthesis he could produce a philosophy which would "reach
farther into the heights and depths of life than the medieval
synthesis; and would yet be immune to the alternate moods
of pessimism and optimism, of cynicism and of sentimentality to which modern culture is now so prone." [25] Further,
he wished to reopen this debate in order to make the Atonement achieve and retain cultural relevance.

Niebuhr said that history has shown a triumph of the
Renaissance emphasis over the Reformation emphasis. Luther's defeatism and Calvin's obscurantism contributed to
this defeat. The general atmosphere of historic optimism of
the past centuries seemed to refute the truth of the Reformation and validate what was both true and false in the Renaissance. Consequently the Reformation emphasis was neglected.

The realization of concomitant good and evil in history
has given the justification aspect of grace a new relevance.
Whenever human goodness and wisdom acknowledge their
limits, justification begins to make sense out of life. The
hopeful periods of history would seem to make the gospel of
grace as justification irrelevant. Periods of disillusionment
make known the vanity of such hopefulness. Niebuhr claimed
that we are now in such a period of disillusionment.

Niebuhr said that the time is ripe for a new synthesis of
the twofold aspects of grace as Power in the light of the
Renaissance and Reformation interpretations. According to
Niebuhr, the Renaissance must make its contribution to this
new synthesis by stressing diligence in the pursuit of proximate answers and solutions. The Renaissance claim that man
is a creature with an unlimited potential is an essential truth
about life and history. But a simple trust in human power
alone is disastrous. To this must be added the Reformation

insight that the fulfillment of life and human perfection are impossibilities of human nature. History can realize only degrees of self-fulfillment. The chief contribution of the Reformation to this new synthesis, then, is its insistence that life is never fulfilled in history either by grace or by the capacities of human nature.

Thus Niebuhr looked upon his theology as a synthesis of justification and sanctification, but a more adequate synthesis than that of medieval Catholicism. Using this double aspect of grace, Niebuhr contended that history is meaningful but depends upon God for its fulfillment.

Niebuhr maintained that the Christian doctrine of the Atonement is the final key to this interpretation. The Atonement, paradoxically relating the divine mercy and wrath, symbolizes the seriousness of history. The significant distinction between good and evil in history is preserved. He said that the "realization of the good must be taken seriously; it is the wheat, separated from the tares, which is gathered 'into my barn,' which is to say that the good within the finite flux has significance beyond that flux." [26] On the other hand, God's mercy points to the corruption of evil in every historic achievement. This divine mercy destroys evil by taking evil into itself.

The Atonement is not a thing anticipated by human wisdom; but once the truth of the Atonement is accepted by faith, it symbolizes all that man can and cannot do. There is no limit to sanctification, Niebuhr wrote, "except of course the one limit, that there will be some corruption, as well as deficiency, of virtue and truth on the new level of achievement." [27]

ESCHATOLOGICAL GRACE

The full completion of man's life awaits a divine action beyond history. Only God can complete man's moral struggle and fulfill his fragmentary existence. History, then, is an

interim between the disclosure of its true norm in Christ and
the perfect fulfillment of its meaning. And, Niebuhr said,
this "interim is characterized by positive corruptions, as well
as by partial realizations and approximations of the meaning
of life." [28] Final sanctification must lie beyond history. History remains under the paradox of grace of Power, fulfilling,
and not fulfilling, the true norm of man until the end of
history. Beyond history the contradiction is overcome by the
mercy of God. This promise of final grace is, so to say, an
eschatological gift.

Faith points to an *end* where all corruptions are overcome.
Niebuhr said that symbolically "this is expressed in the New
Testament in the hope that the suffering Messiah will 'come
again' with 'power and great glory.' Men shall 'see the Son
of man sitting on the right hand of power, and coming in the
clouds of heaven.' " [29] The New Testament eschatological
symbols speak of this end as *telos*. Pointing to the ultimate
from the standpoint of the conditioned, these symbols give an
answer of assurance to counteract the threat and peril of
meaninglessness. The Niebuhr reader is left with some doubt,
however, as to just what kind of reality is designated by
Niebuhr's "eschatological symbol."

Niebuhr said that these eschatological symbols are to be
taken seriously but not literally. He said this is so because
these symbols have a double character. They are meaningful
for history, but they transcend history as spirit transcends
nature. They cannot be reduced to a point in history. They
are meaningful in that (1) they keep the ethical problems of
history clearly defined, and (2) they indicate the nature of
the perfection of history for which grace as Truth established
the norm and grace as Power anticipates fulfillment in experience. When these symbols are taken literally they confuse
the mind of the church, distort the relation between time and
eternity, and reduce God's ultimate vindication over history
to a point in history; for Niebuhr, one such falsification is
expressed in the hope of a millennial age. But to take history
seriously is to take these symbols seriously.

Niebuhr said that the eschatological grace beyond man (*telos*) forms a transhistorical counterpoint to the paradox of grace in history. Yet eschatological grace does not annul the tensions of grace as Power over and in man. Eschatological grace both conforms to and fulfills grace as Power in history. He said that the New Testament "last things" are described in the fundamental symbols of the return of Christ, the last judgment, and the resurrection from the dead. Tracing these three interrelations will give an indication of Niebuhr's view of grace as a final fulfillment of the human condition.

Niebuhr said that the eschatological symbol of the return of Christ guarantees the victory that so often mocks faith. The first coming of Christ defined the true norm of history. This norm cannot ultimately be denied, or life would be meaningless. The faith in the return of the suffering Messiah as triumphant judge and redeemer indicates the confidence that this true norm will be achieved. Niebuhr noted:

> The two most basic ideas in this hope of the "parousia" are that the redemption of the world does not require the destruction of creation since creation is not itself evil, and secondly that redemption must come from God since every human action remains with the contradictions of sin.[30]

Sin makes the triumph of love in history impossible; love remains suffering love. Through faith, however, the Christian apprehends that beyond history love is triumphant. The return of Christ vindicates God's sovereignty and the final supremacy of love.

This final redemption of history is also the culmination of history. Not only does it refute the utopian idea of a simple fulfillment of history, it also refutes the otherworldliness that believes history is robbed of its final meaning in the consummation. The judgment and the resurrection, other aspects of eschatological grace, are subordinate to the return of the triumphant Christ since they are part of the vindication of God in the second coming.

The ethical struggles and contradictions of history are clarified and given meaning at the last judgment. Man is finally judged by the norm of true manhood. According to Niebuhr's account, there are three important facets to the symbol of the last judgment. The first is the idea that Christ, the true norm of history, is the final judge of history. Man will be judged for his self-love on the basis of the norm of Christ's sacrificial love—by the ideal possibility, and not by the contrast between the finite and the eternal character of God.[31] Second, the symbol emphasizes the seriousness of good and evil in history and the gravity of historical decisions. God does not erase the distinction between good and evil in history because of the moral ambiguity of all human actions. Niebuhr used the parable of the wheat and the tares to show that good and evil cannot always be distinguished in history. The final judgment makes a provisional distinction between the degrees of righteousness and unrighteousness among men; but the final judgment then exposes the deep-rooted ambiguity of these provisional distinctions. The righteous know that their self-interest has taken away any final pretension to righteousness. Thirdly, Niebuhr said that the last judgment is at the end of history, showing the double character of all historical striving. No process of growth in history can emancipate man from his sin and free him from judgment. When man confronts God as judge it is sin, not death, which is the real peril.

Niebuhr felt that many modern Christians discredited the idea of a final judgment because of the alleged fires of hell associated with it. Niebuhr said that it was unwise "to claim any knowledge of either the furniture of heaven or the temperature of hell; or to be too certain about any details of the Kingdom of God in which history is consummated. But it is prudent to accept the testimony of the heart, which affirms the fear of judgment." [32]

All man's efforts to redeem and sanctify life are declared meaningful by the resurrection. What man does in history is

significant for eternity. The resurrection preserves and transfigures these efforts into a final harmony. Niebuhr said that
the resurrection (as an eschatological symbol) points to the
harmonious culmination of the tension between spiritual freedom and the nature-finitude dimension of human life. The
resurrection of the body indicates the ultimate harmony of
spirit and nature; it sublimates rather than annuls the historical process. The doctrine of the resurrection affirms that
man cannot consummate history. It denies the hope that human nature is capable and worthy of survival beyond death.
The Christian faith conceives of resurrection as a loving
fellowship with a God who has the power to bring history to
completion.

For Niebuhr, then, the symbols of eschatology express the
faith that God's final act is to perfectly justify and sanctify
history; God's final word to history is the perfect fulfillment
of grace. The *telos* finally destroys the defiance that has
marched through history along with the good. The "Antichrist" will appear at the end of history, and the final victory
of Christ will therefore come not in history but at the end
of history.

V. Love and Justice

There is still a widespread impression abroad in religious circles that although Niebuhr was effective in destroying illusions, he failed to provide adequate positive direction. It is my conviction, however, that out of the resources of the Christian faith he provided a responsible approach to concrete social issues. One of the most fruitful dimensions of his thought is the way he used the resources of faith for achieving a responsible society. His test for true religion was social relevance. Those who claim that there is no basis in his theology for social action either have not read him with care or do not understand the depths of life.

The relation of God's love (agape) to individual and collective life in terms of justice was close to the heart of Niebuhr's thought. He explored intensely the problem of love and justice, and many parts of his theology developed or changed as a result of this exploration. He rescued his theology from the abstract by constantly applying it to specific human problems. It was his conviction that only a Christian, informed and empowered by God's grace, could continue to struggle for a better world without illusions about human nature and the historic process. Niebuhr put it this way in a memorable paragraph:

> Nothing that is worth doing can be achieved in our lifetime; therefore we must be saved by hope. Nothing which is true or beautiful or good makes complete sense in any immediate context of history; therefore we must be saved by faith. Nothing we do, however virtuous, can be accomplished alone; therefore we are saved by love. No virtuous act is quite as virtuous from the standpoint of our friend or foe as it is from our standpoint. Therefore we must be saved by the final form of love which is forgiveness.[1]

The perfect expression of God's grace is the sacrificial love demonstrated by Christ on the Cross. Grace as sacrificial love is the pinnacle of the ethical norm of the Kingdom of God, the moral ideal of the Kingdom. Consequently, grace as the perfect agape of the Cross deals not with static legal norms but with moral dynamics. Assuming that the sinful self has accepted by faith God's grace as Truth (Incarnation and Atonement) and received God's grace as Power (Justification and Sanctification), how is the new self to apply Kingdom ethics (the ethic of the Cross) to secular social structures? Niebuhr answered this question by relating love to the structures of justice. Niebuhr considered the relation of agape to the struggle for justice to be as profound a revelation of the possibilities of God's grace and the limitations imposed by man's sin as any facet of existence. He believed the basic presuppositions of the Christian faith are political on the side of their application. "To deny this," he said, "is to be oblivious of one aspect of historic existence which the Renaissance understood so well: that life represents an indeterminate series of possibilities and therefore of obligations to fulfill them." [2] His theology flowed naturally toward political reflection and action.

He was concerned that love be defined in such a way that it had meaning for the structures of justice. He said that the church is responsible for relating God's love in a realistic way to the moral problems of an industrial civilization, but, unfortunately, modern Christianity is characterized by a lack of ethical relevancy.

> The fact is that more men in our modern era are irreligious because religion has failed to make civilization ethical than because it has failed to maintain its intellectual respectability. For every person who disavows religion because some ancient and unrevised dogma outrages his intelligence, several become irreligious because the social impotence of religion outrages their conscience.[3]

The church and individual Christians are too often guilty of substituting benevolence for justice in the basic organizations of life. Love is frequently defined by Christians only in terms of personal relations.

THE AGAPE OF THE CROSS

The unmeasured love of Christ the Truth (sacrificial, heedless, uncalculating) sets the norm for man's life. This love judges man's actions and finds them to be lacking. Because of the atoning sacrifice of Christ, God's grace as Power both forgives man for falling short of love and provides the moral undergirding for him to remain faithful to love. Justification releases man to a life of love, and sanctification empowers him with grace to reach levels of love that would otherwise be impossible. This is the relationship of love to the moral life of the regenerate Christian.

Niebuhr's social ethics grew out of this love of the Cross. Because of man's indeterminate freedom, only love can be the norm for his social nature. Man is free *in order* that he might love. However, any realistic approach to social issues must recognize the power struggle that pervades society and the resulting necessity of force. When moral achievements in the social order are judged on the basis of the divine perfection of love, they are shown to be inadequate. Niebuhr was able to relate love to the social struggle by the original relation of God's love to his justice in the paradox of the Atonement. In the Cross God reveals both his wrath and his love. God's love is revealed by his taking wrath upon himself. This original source of the relation of love to justice in the Atonement was used by Niebuhr in all of his ethical constructions for the social order.

Niebuhr viewed the application of love to social relations as an "impossible possibility." This phrase expressed Niebuhr's way of saying that love is always relevant, but its perfect attainment in social life is difficult. (He later abandoned this phrase, not because of its inaccuracy, but because it was so easily misunderstood.) The transcendence of the love ideal makes it an impossibility, while the constant improvement of every human achievement by the love ethic makes it a possibility. Love is relevant in that it provides judgment for man's actions and the spring for ethical motives. At the same time, love is impossible as a wholly adequate social ethic. When love is most fully attained, at that moment it is in danger of corruption. The insights derived from the soul's encounter with God must be incorporated into institutions which can know nothing of such an encounter. Insights from individual religious experience must provide the collective man with proper inspiration for action.[4]

Niebuhr felt that love is not a simple possibility in social relations because perfect love is always crucified in history. He held that the primary meaning of love is to be found in self-sacrifice (and was accused by his brother Richard, among others, of defining love too narrowly). He said that it is the failure to take account of this crucifixion that has brought confusion into the modern application of love to the social structure. Without this love, however, progress would be impossible. Some degree of heedless love must always be present, or else the giver of love will end in resentment about the possible absence of perfect reciprocity in the recipient of his love. Every form of moral advance is ultimately dependent upon love for its direction and motive. Religious faith is the motive for seeking the moral life. Although the relationship between the ethic of love (or the Kingdom of God) and concrete social action was viewed uneasily by Niebuhr, he nevertheless struggled to relate the two.

THE RELATION OF LOVE AND JUSTICE

Agape is related to social action in terms of dynamic ethical principles. Niebuhr maintained that love is under obligation to accept the best principles it can for the ordering of society. Often it is necessary to give priority to one principle over another. One such general principle is justice. Justice is not distinctively Christian, but agape cannot repeal it or work apart from it. Love commonly means the self's active care for another; justice commonly means the impartial consideration of all parties concerned without special interest or personal preferences. Justice is the mediating principle between absolute love and the power principles of society—the relative embodiment of love in social structures. For large groups the highest goal is justice rather than love.

The relation between love and justice is dialectical. Justice is love in realizable action. God's love for us (agape) leads us to love one another (mutual love). Mutual love needs agape to keep it from selfishness. Mutual love is one notch below the level of agape, while one notch below mutual love is justice (the only reachable norm for society). The minimal level of justice is the life needs of the neighbor that speak to the self as "claims" and "rights." Justice is a moral concept that is used by reason to discriminate the needs due the neighbor. Justice is the attempt to institutionalize the moral demands of love. Niebuhr put the relation this way:

> Systems and principles of justice are the servants and instruments of the spirit of brotherhood in so far as they extend the sense of obligation towards the other, (a) from an immediately felt obligation, prompted by obvious need, to a continued obligation expressed in fixed principles of mutual support; (b) from a simple relation

of the self and one "other" to the complex relations of the self and the "others"; and (c) finally from the obligations . . . which the community defines from its more impartial perspective.[5]

When justice is applied to the community, it becomes a principle of balance between competing groups within the community. For Niebuhr, equal justice, an inexact term covering a wide range of ideas, was generally defined as a decent equilibrium of power.

Niebuhr's insistence on the balance of power was important for his community policy. This idea is well presented in the following passage:

> Justification by faith in the realm of justice means that we will not regard the pressures and counterpressures, the tensions, the overt and covert conflicts by which justice is achieved and maintained as normative in the absolute sense; but neither will we ease our conscience by seeking to escape from involvement in them. We will know that we cannot purge ourselves of the sin and guilt in which we are involved by the moral ambiguities of politics without also disavowing responsibility for creative possibilities of justice.[6]

Equality, then, governs the idea of justice. Moral pragmatism is inevitable in righting social wrongs. Since community relations have limited morality and reason (self-interest is the primary datum of groups), power must be countered by power. Thus Niebuhr backed the formation of trade unions because he felt that workers had to organize to protect themselves against the exploitive tendencies of a laissez-faire economy and its power wielders. He also backed Roosevelt's New Deal because he felt that basic social security required the assistance of government, that is, political power checking economic power. Or again, he saw the black citizens' human rights fight making a wise use of social and political power to gain equal dignity and redress old grievances. But the government, as an instrument of distributive justice, was also a power that had to be watched and corrected.

On the international level, the same pragmatic balance of power was necessary for Niebuhr. Communist Russia and China, doggedly hauling peasant societies into a twentieth-century technological age with a totalitarian grip, were in the hands of political elites vulnerable to the abuse of their power. Communist evil, Niebuhr said, resulted from its monopoly of power (absolute power over other men producing evils worse than injustice), its utopianism (attribution of the source of evil to something outside man—private property), its faith in revolution (a substitute religion), and its dogmatism (ideology masquerading as science). For example, in the autumn 1956 Suez crisis, Niebuhr objected to the Eisenhower-Dulles policy because he felt its "legalistic-moralistic approach" played into the hands of the Soviets and strengthened Nasser's intransigence. Communist ideology, claiming righteous purity with religious zeal, generated an imperialism dangerous to the West and its protector, the United States. Niebuhr felt that it was necessary for U.S. foreign policy to place limits on the expansionist zeal of Communist nations. At the same time America was too eager to impose its democratic traditions on developing countries not yet ready for them, Niebuhr said. Add to this zeal other major miscalculations, and the anguish of Vietnam was the result. Since the struggle between the major powers will be with us for decades to come, he felt that a wise statecraft must take into account the collective egoisms of nations and the ideal of a tolerable mutuality. The major world powers must exercise their responsibility for world order while refraining from exploiting their advantaged position.

When love goes into action in society, it gives rise to specific schemes or principles of justice. Justice is a second best to prevent one life from taking advantage of another. A realistic approach will take into account the tendency of man to think more highly of himself than he ought to think. Love cannot be an alternative to the "pushing and shoving" which justice requires. Political structures and pressures remain necessary. Although justice may be the approximation of brotherhood under conditions of sin, Niebuhr said that we need a great deal of this "second-rate" Christianity.

Niebuhr said that modern culture too easily assumes that the level of sanctification in the life of the individual can be regarded as a simple possibility for social groups. He contended that the will to power is a threat to the sanctification of even the most intimate groups. This celebrated "moral man and immoral society" theme runs through his writings, as already noted. It argues that a sharp distinction must be drawn between "the moral and social behavior of individuals and of social groups, national, racial, and economic; and that this distinction justifies and necessitates political policies which a purely individualistic ethic must always find embarrassing." [7] The larger the group, the greater the difficulty in attaining justice.

Niebuhr said that the question of what is right in love and justice is usually clear. The real problem is what is possible in the light of man's self-centeredness and intransigence. Hence Niebuhr argued for the principle of prudence. The application of love to schemes of justice must prudently take account of the human factor. Where group loyalties are involved, for example, coercion is often the only means of attaining justice. This holds true even for those men who most adequately embody agape. Love, persuasion, reason, and insight may mitigate and transcend the social struggle, but they cannot eliminate it. He said that this "is the very heart of the problem of Christian politics: the readiness to use power and interest in the service of an end dictated by love and yet an absence of complacency about the evil inherent in them." [8]

Niebuhr's application of love to the social struggle came by way of a long and searching criticism of four major approaches. These positions are: (1) Protestant pietistic individualism. This position sees no necessity of applying love to justice. (2) A vague Christian or secular moralism (both

Marxism and liberalism). This group tries to apply love
directly to justice without taking account of original sin.
(3) Roman Catholicism's natural law theory. This view rele-
gates love to the realm of perfection while the church rationally defines the nature of Christian justice. The error here is
an uncritical regard for the purity of reason. (4) The socialist Christian position. This position applies the insights of
socialism to society, but submits them to the criticism of the
law of love. Niebuhr found in these positions the way that
love should *not* be related to justice; he excluded these various alternatives.

Love is related to justice in that it partly fulfills and partly
negates justice. Niebuhr developed this relationship on three
levels. (1) Love is the source of the norms of justice. From
the love of Christ come suggested possibilities for improving
justice. Equality is a significant principle of justice deduced
from the law of love and implicit within the love command:
"Thus equality is love in terms of logic." [9] Or again, the
ability to enter sympathetically into the experience of another
turns out to be another form of love that is close to agape.
This Niebuhr called "imaginative justice." Forms of justice
can never attain to agape, but they can approximate it. (2)
Love is the dynamic motive for the establishment of justice.
Love is constantly suggesting means to raise justice to higher
levels of purity by the inspiration of agape. Reason cannot
do this because it is subject to the corruptions of self-interest.
How does love inspire justice? When the self encounters the
agape of God, it responds in contrition and gratitude. Man's
contrite recognition of his sinfulness enhances justice because
it establishes a foundation for better harmony in communal
life. When man encounters agape he is grateful for the goodness of life. It is good because God created it, and this in
turn validates the devoted efforts to achieve higher forms of
justice. This gratitude springing from agape is a powerful
dynamic. (3) Love is an end, while justice is a means. Love
is the final goal toward which justice moves. Justice is not

a fully satisfactory goal in itself because it falls short of love, being dependent upon coercive power on the one hand, and requiring rational calculations in the balancing of rights against rights on the other. In comparison, love is free, creative, and redemptive.

Niebuhr's position may be summarized by saying that love is the operating motive in seeking the best possible social order, while justice is the instrument of love's application. Justice may approximate love, but it is always capable of being corrected by love and raised to a higher level. Love fulfills justice insofar as it draws justice into greater and greater achievements of brotherhood. Love negates justice in that justice has elements which contradict love on each new level of achievement. Love can always raise justice to new heights; its possibility of transforming justice is indeterminate. Thus love requires, negates, and fulfills justice.

JUSTICE AND THE PARADOX OF GRACE

Niebuhr felt that the struggle for justice reveals the limitations of sin and the possibilities of progress by God's grace in society. Love is the norm for individual life; brotherhood is the norm for social existence. Progress can be made from one generation to another although progress is fraught with danger. Because man is a free creature there are no limits to the purity of brotherhood he may reach; but because of man's freedom his brotherhood is never safe from corruption on each new level of achievement. Brotherhood is faced with the indeterminate character of both good and evil (thus making society dynamic).

Niebuhr's doctrine of human nature determined his views of what can be accomplished in attaining brotherhood in society. His view of man caused him to seek proximate solutions rather than absolute ones. This approach avoided the idolatrous fanaticisms which accompany absolute solutions and released constructive elements. His vocation was to clear the path for hopeful solutions by first destroying the illusions which flourished among religious and secular liberals and intellectuals. Events largely helped him to win this battle, and it is now easier to see the constructive side of his thought.

Original sin and the paradox of grace are as true expressions of social life and the struggle for justice as they are of the life of the individual. Niebuhr's doctrine of justification indicated his awareness of the difficulty of relating agape to social action. (1) Justification points to the source of motive and morale for ethical living amidst the sinfulness of the human situation; it permits the Christian to participate in struggles for justice without making the struggle the norm. Justification enables the Christian to act morally in a sinful world even though this act involves participation in the evil which produces conflicts of conscience. The Christian is never satisfied that a particular strategy is the will of God. (2) Further, by making man conscious of his ethical responsibilities, the doctrine of justification keeps man from having a self-righteous conscience. The righteous and the idealists, secure in their own virtue, are those most in need of justification. Because they feel no need of justification they are unbending and uncreative in their approach to the unrighteous. (3) All efforts at justice are equally far from the Kingdom of God because they involve coercive efforts and coercion is foreign to the brotherhood of love. In this sense, "all have sinned and fall short of the glory of God" (Rom. 3:23). Here Niebuhr's doctrine of the "equality of sin and the inequality of guilt" is transferred from the individual to the group.[10] When man's righteousness is set over against God's righteousness, the need for justification in the social struggle is obvious.

Justification, and its resultant humility, is the step prior to sanctification in social life just as it is in individual life. In the area of the relatively good and evil it is important to recognize that there are always higher possibilities of sanctification in every historic situation. Christians are under obligation to establish "indeterminate degrees" of justice in the social order, but they must do so in the light of the doctrine of justification. The recognition of the need for justification in the social order leads to greater degrees of sanctification. Niebuhr said that sanctification "in the realm of social relations demands recognition of the impossibility of perfect sanctification." [11]

Human society as well as the individual can know the sanctifying power of grace. Niebuhr ascribed to human communities and social institutions the possibility of renewal through grace. Although sanctification in the life of communities and social institutions is not so clearly defined an experience as it is in the individual, Niebuhr said that old forms and structures of life may be renewed rather than destroyed by the vicissitudes of history. This possibility, he held, "establishes the validity of the Christian doctrine of life through death for the collective, as well as for the individual, organism." [12]

The Renaissance insight of the possibility of indefinite moral improvement does not mean that Niebuhr returned to a liberal philosophy of progress for the social order. He saw an apocalyptic pattern in history in which good does not overcome evil in history but grows alongside it to the end. Both Renaissance and Reformation possibilities form a constant tension throughout history; sanctification is possible, but never without justification. At the same time, the "paradox of grace" saves the Christian from pessimism. To point out the limits of man's existence does not mean a negation of that existence. Pessimism is just as much a result of expecting too much as of expecting too little. The same mind that is given the grace to know its sin is also given the grace to know its possibilities. Niebuhr's analysis may perplex, but it does not lead to despair.

Niebuhr was a critic of the pessimist and cynic. From his earliest writings he warned against a too consistent realism. He was vocal in his criticism of those who recognize only man's limitations and do not do justice to man's indeterminate possibilities. He put it this way:

> The cynic who discounts the moral potentialities of human nature seems always to verify his critical appraisal of human nature for the reason that his very skepticism lowers the moral potentialities of the individuals and groups with which he deals. On the other hand, the faith that assumes generosity in the fellow man is also verified because it tends to create what it assumes.[13]

He was critical of both cynicism and utopianism; he attempted to take a position between the two. When the illusions of cynicism and utopianism are stripped away, there are endless possibilities for perfecting the justice of social institutions.

The conclusion most abhorrent to Niebuhr's critics was his idea that the growth of man's possibilities for good carries with it the possibility of growth in evil. This conclusion leaves no room for a perfect society. But contrary to the opinion of Niebuhr's critics, his thought was as far from cynicism as it was from utopianism. He said that it is wrong to interpret reality in the terms of either approach. He wrote:

> An attitude which avoids both sentimentality and cynicism must obviously be grounded in a Christian view of human nature which is schooled by the Gospel not to take the pretensions of men at their face value, on the one hand, and, on the other, not to deny the residual capacity for justice among even sinful men.[14]

Niebuhr attempted to arrive at an operating optimism, a balanced position between extremes. There was no defeatism for Niebuhr in the Christian faith. The Christian faith sees man realistically in his sinfulness; but it also sees God's grace giving man the power to meet life's needs in a confident, victorious spirit. He said that mankind "will finally find political instruments and moral resources adequate for a wholesome communal life on a world-wide scale." [15]

Far from being a defeatist, Niebuhr may even have had

underlying strains of utopianism or perfectionism in his thought. Utopians are buoyed up by their expectations; Niebuhr's hopeful expectations were more sober, but they were important for his thought on moral conduct. John Bennett said it is probably true "that the vigor of Niebuhr's attacks on perfectionism comes partly from the fact that he has always been much tempted by it." [16] Niebuhr preserved certain perfectionist elements in his statement of the gospel: in his interpretation of love and of Christ's "powerlessness" in history and in the tribute he paid to perfectionistic pacifism. On the other hand, he never gave a final picture of society—no complete vision of the world order, no "brave new world"—because of the tragic character of the political act.

LOVE, JUSTICE, AND THE COMMUNITY OF GRACE

Niebuhr loved the church (and made no apology for being critical of it), gave it devoted service (from pastor in Detroit to leader in the ecumenical movement), and wrote extensively for and about it in his periodical writings. He had a great deal to say about the functions of the church in its worship, sacraments, polity, etc., but here we are interested in how he viewed the church in relation to the social order. The first business of the church in society, he said, is "to raise and answer religious questions within the framework of which . . . the moral issues must be solved." [17] His concern led him to deliver some withering blasts at churchmen who neglected the problem of social justice. His controversy with the European theologian Karl Barth was an evidence of his feeling. He thought (1) that Barth's theology insulated the church from the world, (2) that Barth was too eschatological for calculated political decisions, (3) that Barth was so pragmatic that he disavowed all moral principles, and (4) that Barth isolated Christianity from the effects of philosophical and scientific speculation.

Niebuhr had a continuously growing appreciation for the church, but he did not want this appreciation to betray him into complacency about the new evil that could come into being through the church. Reminding the church that it was still subject to the judgment of God, he said that "every vehicle of God's grace, the preacher of the word, the prince of the church, the teacher of theology, the historic institution, the written word, the sacred canon, all these are in danger of being revered as if they were themselves divine." [18] He never hesitated to catalog the sins of the church, but his primary accusation was that the church had failed to render a service in the cause of social justice. He wrote that the church "maintains ethical attitudes in the interstices of our civilization, but does not build them into its structure. It embroiders life with its little amenities, but it does not change the pattern." [19] The church is frequently indifferent to the immediate problems of relative justice. Christian leaders flee their daily responsibilities and decisions of justice in human affairs. "Yesterday they discovered that the church may be an ark in which to survive a flood. Today they seem so enamored of this special function of the church that they have decided to turn the ark into a home on Mount Ararat and live in it perpetually." [20] Niebuhr said it is a tragedy that the church cultivates its spirituality by divorcing itself from an understanding of the brutal elements of collective life. He felt that the orthodox church convicts men of only the secondary sins of society, while the liberal church is unable to convict men of sin at all because of its romantic view of human nature.

Ideally, the church offers both diagnosis and healing to a sub-Christian culture. Why, then, has the church failed to grapple with the real moral problems of life? Niebuhr maintained that dozens of reasons may be given, but he settled on one "real case." He said that there seems to be a natural incompatibility between every high cause and the agency which advances it. Even the church cannot escape this paradox. The chief example of the error of "regarding the historic church as the unqualified representative of Christ on earth so that the enemies of the church become the enemies of God" [21] was called by Niebuhr the "Catholic heresy." The Catholic church considers itself the extension of the Incarnation and assures men of their salvation if they can climb a "ladder of merit." At the same time Niebuhr said that the evangelical churches, coupling pietism and perfectionist illusions, are tempted to disregard the moral ambiguity in the life of the redeemed. The less democratic churches have an inherent danger of pride and the abuse of power. On the other hand, the sectarian churches are not powerful and resourceful enough to maintain a Christian witness in the struggle for justice in the social situation.

Niebuhr singled out Billy Graham as a personable and honorable exponent of pietistic evangelicalism. Niebuhr had a high appreciation of Graham as a Christian and as an evangelist. But, said Niebuhr, Graham's representative pietistic moralism does not bring the Christian faith into correspondence with our social obligations, nor does it recognize the precariousness of the virtues of the redeemed. This pietism, ignoring the perplexities of guilt and responsibility which Christians must face, thinks that the problems of an atomic age can be solved simply by converting people to Christ; it lacks the grace to measure the distance between man's fragmentary righteousness and the divine holiness. Niebuhr felt that this individualistic approach to faith and commitment was in danger of obscuring the highly complex task of justice in the community. On the other hand, he said that the message of Billy Graham, despite its simple pietism and obscurantist framework of "The Bible says . . . ," has "preserved something of the biblical sense of a divine judgment and mercy before which all human strivings and ambitions are convicted of guilt and reduced to their proper proportions." [22]

For Niebuhr the first business of the church was to raise and answer the religious question about the meaning of existence. Within this framework the moral-political issues which man faces must be solved. He had a firm conviction that the church can take its gospel of love seriously and apply it to the basic problems of life in this world. He affirmed that the church is always a genuine source of grace, whatever might be its corruptions. The church is founded upon faith in God; in spite of the historical corruptions into which it has fallen it bears the "oracles of God." It is the community where "the Kingdom of God impinges most unmistakably upon history because it is the community where the judgment and the mercy of God are known, piercing through all the pride and pretensions of men and transforming their lives." [23]

The church, when it combines two qualities, makes the gospel effective in moral-political life. These qualities are spiritual vigor and social intelligence. By the grace of God *in* man the new creature is given a powerful religious devotion that keeps the strong forces of the self in check. A genuine "crucifixion" of the self, a new birth, gives spiritual vigor. The humble person who arises as a result of this regenerating experience has a good chance of being a mediator of the divine grace and presenting the gospel in its full dimensions to the social order. Religious fervor creates the will to live the Christian life in all its ramifications. The full substance of the new life in Christ "and of the church as a community of grace is maintained by the continual renewal of the faith through the Scriptures." [24] A spiritual rebirth combined with educated guidance make a potent working force for a realistic approach.

What is this realistic approach? Niebuhr said that it is the recognition of original sin and the paradox of grace in society as well as in the individual. It is the recognition that reconciling love eases and qualifies but does not destroy the relative injustices of society. The church's effort in the cause of reconciliation is advanced when it creates Christian realists who know that justice requires conflict. There are plenty of moral idealists in the church who confuse the issue by thinking that they can establish justice in a simple manner.

This approach demands that the church make a twofold honest analysis: (1) The church must help people make a self-analysis through the preaching of judgment. Men know how selfish they are when they are scrutinized from the perspective of the absolute, and this must come before society can be healed by grace.[25] Such preaching involves a pitiless analysis of the motives and self-justification of man. (2) The church must also make a rigorous analysis of society for its members because most Christians do not know the kind of world they live in. Niebuhr said that it "is only in rare cases that moral good-will makes itself effective automatically. It must be directed." [26]

What are the consequences of this realistic approach? On the one hand the church can mitigate the social struggle; on the other hand it may transcend the social struggle by destroying conceit. The gospel produces a spirit of humility and repentance. For Niebuhr, nothing was more socially relevant than humility born of faith's encounter. Humility, rooted in repentance, expresses itself in the spirit of forgiveness. The righteousness of any just cause, though real, is not absolute. The church can make an invaluable gift to society by presenting to the community a greater number of contrite souls who express their redemption partly in the recognition of the remnant of pride that remains in the soul of every redeemed person. "Mercy to the foe is possible only to those who know themselves to be sinners." [27]

The church may also transcend the social struggle. As well as creating a spirit of love, the church can create an attitude of trust and faith toward other human beings, thus stressing the potentialities of man rather than the immediate realities. "Through such imagination the needs of the social foe are appreciated, his inadequacies are understood in the light of his situation, and his possibilities for higher and more moral action are recognized." [28]

Niebuhr's discussion of the church and social justice assumed the doctrines of sin and grace in all of their ramifications. The church is composed of repentant sinners who have
been born again through the grace of God. "The church is
created not by the righteousness of the pharisee but the contrition of the publican; not by the achievement of pure goodness but by the recognition of the sinfulness of all human
goodness." [29] Part of the message of the church is a message
of repentance, but it must be repentance for the saints as well
as for those who deny the Lord.

The church, then, is composed of those persons who have
recognized their sinfulness in the light of Christ the Truth.
These persons have, through repentance and faith, been given
grace as Power to live the new life in Christ. These saints
remain in need of justifying grace because they are not
perfectly sanctified. The church as an institution shares in
this paradox. The problem of the church is to retain the
paradox of grace. The church must absorb what is valid in
the Renaissance attitude toward history and yet retain the
Reformation emphasis on the equal need of all men for
divine forgiveness. This attitude will not cause the church
to encourage simple answers to the complex problems of
society.

In the final analysis, then, the message of the church must
be eschatological. The church is the eschatological community because it knows that its consummation is at the end
of history. When the church is not sufficiently eschatological,
it is in danger of becoming an Antichrist. This is not to
exclude the redemptive act of God; but the church must keep
eyes fixed steadfastly on the final goal, for in that goal is
found the criterion for the message of the church to society.
The most relevant task of the church is to proclaim the
classical Christian gospel.

VI. Relevance and the
March of Time

Mind-boggling events have taken place since Niebuhr died in 1971: the deaths of Harry Truman and Lyndon Johnson, Richard Nixon's tragic Watergate crisis, war in the Middle East, rapprochement with Red China and an uneasy détente with Soviet Russia, the energy crisis, large-scale unemployment, an escalating crime rate in the nation, the erosion of confidence in the leadership of the Western world, and the emergence of a new crop of politicians on the national scene. As the long-time interpreter of twentieth-century American religious and political life, Niebuhr would be at home in our era.

Only recently have Niebuhr quotations begun once again to sprinkle the political speeches of national office seekers and the pages of learned religious journals. Niebuhr has been neglected for a decade. During the great theological slump of the 1960s, when theologies of "play" and of the "death of God" were anticipating a "swinging" Kingdom of God now, Niebuhr was scorned by the Dionysiac revelers. At the same time, the New Left (now the old New Left) in politics, persuaded by the rhetoric of its own simplistic radicalism which seemed to call for burning down or bringing down everything, concluded that Niebuhr's Christian realism was a sellout to the establishment. As the fads of the '60s are forgotten, Niebuhr is being studied with a new intensity. Today's backward glance at Niebuhr is permitting us to see that he was not just a representative of the cold war of the 1950s. The resources in his thought go beyond his response to any one period of history, and events since his retirement have not refuted the main outlines of his Christian realism. Just as those of us who were young twenty years ago learned from Niebuhr, so today's young can profit from the way he applied the Christian faith to modern experience.

What can Niebuhr say to a new generation of theologians and statesmen? Is he even needed today by either church or world? I have obviously written this book as a Niebuhr partisan, and you would expect me to say, "Niebuhr remains relevant." But among my plaudits, I have also said that some of Niebuhr's ideas and actions were flawed and are now dated. He was often a step ahead of history, but he also made some wrong choices. Niebuhr himself was the first to admit that he was not a painstaking theologian, that he left many aspects of Christian thought undeveloped, and that he made some serious political miscalculations—to which confessions plenty of his critics agreed. In retrospect, some of those who regretted his influence are beginning to see that neither his theology nor his politics were as outrageous as much that has recently come along, and that much of what Niebuhr had to say is anything but obsolete.

Niebuhr was a turning-point figure in American religious history. Since we can't agree with everything he said or did, what can we learn from him? Among the many themes we might consider, I would underscore at least five.

(1) He was equally thinker and doer. His intellectual and physical vitality alone do not explain this combination, because he continued in both worlds during years of physical illness. He consciously tried to overcome the arrogance inher-

ent in pure thought or full-time action by sharing both worlds and speaking with sympathy and authority to each. His life-style offers us an example in how to combine deep yet prag-matic piety. Niebuhr said, "The lives of many intellectuals are boring." He was one of the great contributors to the thinking of our time, but his significance is greater because he did more than think. He was a visible sacrament. Many of the most influential theologians in Christian history have been activists. Contemplative reflection is thus only one of the valid models for the theologian.

The glory of American theology has been its ability to combine faith and practice. European ecclesiastical scholar-ship has seldom understood this best and most durable feature of the American Protestant tradition. Even when Europeans have recognized this American pragmatism, they have failed to appreciate it (and thereby exposed their own intellectual provincialism). Niebuhr entered into an appreciative yet criti-cal conversation with secular thought because of his deep religious commitment. It was solely because of his religious conversion that he joined the political wars and made avail-able the great Christian theological tradition to the American political debate. A generation before the existential Now theologians were shouting it from the front lines, he knew that the safest place for the Christian thinker was in the midst of the social struggle.

At this point a warning should be given: Niebuhr's reli-gious faith cannot be separated from his political activity. Those secular disciples of Niebuhr ("atheists for Niebuhr") who accept his political stance but scorn or ignore his reli-gious experience are mistaken; they violate his own sense of integrity. He claimed that the root of his political faith (both the reflective and the active side) was grounded in his Chris-tian faith. In a recent book, writer Paul Merkley says, "It seems to me that those of Niebuhr's admirers who embrace Niebuhr's political credo without embracing his theological presuppositions owe us some explanation. Niebuhr's own

politics cannot at any point be disengaged—even for purposes
of passing discussion on its 'appropriateness' or its 'relevance'—from his theology." [1] Niebuhr shows us that there
is a theological tradition available to the American intellectual
which the secularist fails to appreciate. He shows that the
secularist takes our political institutions for granted while
ignoring the logic of theology—that political discussion depends upon justice, that justice depends upon ethics, and
that ethics is grounded in theology. The danger remains that
secularists will develop from Niebuhr's political realism an
ethic that is little more than a reflection of the exigencies of
the American strategy in its confrontation with Russia or
China.

(2) Again, we can learn from Niebuhr to define the basic
sin as pride rather than sensuality. Niebuhr's contribution
here can scarcely be overestimated. Not since St. Augustine's
City of God have we had a theologian who so shifted the locus
of sin from the visible misuse of natural impulses to the
more subtle area of man's inflated self-assertion that hides
behind claims of moral disinterestedness and superiority.
Niebuhr gave a sustained and brilliant analysis of both individual and collective egoism. Traditional American moralism
and pietism owe him a permanent debt of gratitude for his
reflections on the nature of sin. His use of the category of
pride was truly devastating in laying bare the inordinate self-
regard that routine propriety so often simply camouflaged.

At this point another warning is important: Niebuhr's category of sensuality—a slothful retreat into unconscious
organicism—should not be overlooked. Sin as pride cannot
be explained apart from sensuality. Niebuhr taught that
man is in a dialectical relationship between spirit and nature,
and sin is always two-dimensional. He focused his attention
upon the cool hypocrisy of the powerful classes, but he was
aware of the growing tendency of the affluent to retreat into
passivity, to want only to be left alone. Self-forgetfulness, a
retreat from the barricades, was the underdeveloped side of

his doctrine of sin. In our day we are probably more conscious than Niebuhr was in his that self-surrender, sloth, and inordinate self-humiliation need to be emphasized as much as pride to fully understand man's sin. Modern society in its accelerating withdrawal into affluent pleasantness needs the category of sensuality to interpret its self-ignoring life. Our generation of backlash and resentment is as tempted by despair as by false optimism.

(3) We can learn from Niebuhr that sin persists on every level of individual achievement, social or cultural advance, and religious pretension. This may be Niebuhr's major warning to both the guardians of the *status quo* and the revolutionaries seeking a new order. Our decade has not outlived Niebuhr's insight that personal and social sanctification are not easily achieved, that we are not as good as we think we are, that only God is sufficient, and that there remains a tension between justice and love. We still need his genius to see that human behavior is complex, that demonic possibilities are built into church and social structures, that human pride and spiritual arrogance rise to new heights precisely at the point where they are closest to the Kingdom of God, and that advance brings vulnerability to new temptations. Since overweening self-regard is ubiquitous, religious and political groups need Niebuhr's caution about special arrogance, about the self-righteous smoke screen laid down by the powerful, and about cheap grace. Just now in theology we are giving reason another chance to cope with sin through technological ingenuity, as for example, when we try to find technocratic solutions for the hunger problem (let's feed everyone without taking away from anyone). Again, reason is showing the folly of the nuclear arms race, that it is foolish to destroy an enemy if the consequence is self-destruction. The sane mind knows that an ever-accelerating arms race can lead only to disaster. But here Niebuhr would remind us that technology and political science take place within power blocs that rarely reform on their own, and those who cherish

reason must realize its limited ability to curb egoism. For
Niebuhr, reason was ambivalent, capable both of checking
sinfulness and of justifying sinfulness.

At this point a third warning is in order: Niebuhr was not
a pessimist about man's possibilities. He taught that by the
grace of God history is full of "indeterminate possibilities"
and that there are no limits on the achievement of a more
universal brotherhood. For him the danger of retrogression
was ever present, but he was prepared to deal with individual
problems with a hopeful openness. All achievements are limited by egoism, he said, but this is no excuse for fatalistic
complacency. "All things are possible" qualifies human sinfulness at every level. Niebuhr would urge us on to ever-
greater measures of responsibility in social and political
affairs. He gave us a worthy model in his own continued
fight for justice for oppressed groups. He placed enormous
emphasis upon human freedom and the possibilities of human life. No one else has been more successful than he at
solving some of our cruel problems. Fortified by the past,
his pilgrim theology was always open to the future.

(4) We can learn from Niebuhr how to be ruggedly realistic about our illusions and those of others. He practiced a
searching self-criticism and self-evaluation and was forever
on the lookout for wrong-headedness in himself and others.
He was as hard on the cynical as he was on the peddlers of
self-satisfaction and triumphalism. This meant for Niebuhr
that he wore his honors lightly. He was not everyone's favorite, but he was popular in some circles because he was not
concerned with popularity. He was no one's uncritical ally.
He retained a sense of humor about his own pretensions, and
he was prepared at times to make a frank reversal of opinion: he had the courage to change. In his old age, for example, he regretted the polemics of his younger days, admitting,
"My polemics were of an impatient young man who had
certain things to say and wanted to get them said clearly
and forcefully. However, I learned a few things as I got

older. . . . I do reject my polemical attitude of the past." [2]
Or again, Niebuhr began his ministry during the crisis of
Western capitalism and was confronted with the utopianism
of Communism and its claim that violence was the only means
to social justice. He was tempted by this view but soon saw
that hate was the same on the left as on the right. His
honesty early led him to reject the butcheries of the Lenin-
Stalin era and to assert that Communism was as close to
barbarism as Fascism. He embodied one of his own favorite
phrases, "self-transcendence."

A fourth warning: Niebuhr suppressed the tendency toward
utopianism in his day, but utopianism is no longer a mortal
sin in our decade. An American Protestant return to the
optimism of the Social Gospel is improbable, but one of the
most arresting features of this last quarter of the twentieth
century is our preoccupation with the future. The Age of
Aquarius has produced visionaries both inside and outside the
church, theologies of hope, and politics of the future. Vision
and realism need each other in our day of rising expectations.
Both the soft utopians (who believe evil can be transformed
by loving persuasion) and the hard utopians (who would
forcefully sacrifice people now for future goals) need Niebuhr's analysis of their illusions.

The scourge of overconfidence always distorts the indeterminate possibilities of history. Niebuhr's emphasis on
justification (the continuation of sin in the life of the redeemed) is a healthy balance to the latest emphasis on sanctification. Eschatological political theologies ("theologies of
liberation") associated with the names of Pannenberg, Molt-
mann, Metz, Alvez, and Braaten, among others, lend themselves to the idea of perfection in history and could well
profit from a measure of Niebuhr's realism. His realism can
also be an antidote to the arrogance of political radicalism.
The necessity of competing for power leaves no group sin-
less; the political act is always tragic. To the soft utopians
(perfection will emerge in history) he would point out that

the distribution of power must be dealt with, and he would
caution hard utopians (evil is morally justified if it brings
about the good) about the abuses of power even by the best
intentioned.

(5) We can learn from Niebuhr something about how to
communicate the gospel in a secular age. John C. Bennett
said that Niebuhr was one of the most persuasive preachers
of this century, and that there are many people today who
are Christians because of his preaching. Bennett illustrated
by saying that there "are two theologians of wide influence
whom I have in mind. One told me that he was converted to
the Christian faith by Niebuhr's preaching when he was a
student, and the other told me half seriously that at the time
he really believed in God because God was necessary for
Reinie's system. This man has since written his own book
about God." [3] Niebuhr was a remarkable "apologetic evangelist," Bennett said. "He won people to the Christian faith
and preserved them in it by showing them how it illumined
the very issues that troubled them most and how it could be
the commitment that might give form to their lives." [4]

With the exception of Paul Tillich, no other theologian of
this century has struck so deeply into the secular mind. Niebuhr was accorded an esteem by the secularists as notable
as that given him by his theological peers. Apart from his
eloquence, how did he do it? He went back to Christian
basics. He took seriously the biblical revelation that God is
revealed in Christ. He was bibliocentric without being bibli-
olatrous. Learning from the past, he applied Christian tradition to secular discussion. He assumed in his evangelistic
apologetics that God is a necessary companion in the human
pilgrimage, and human life makes better sense with him than
without him. He felt that his vocation was to make this
good news credible (intellectual exploits under the direction
of faith), and preaching was an avenue to express the gospel
(his sermons are still widely read). He had the rare gift
of relating ideas to circumstances, and felt that his particular

apologetic task was to show the relevance of the Christian revelation to the hard problems of history. The particular channel he chose was a prophetic interpretation of Christian ethics (and thereby fastened the term "Christian realism" on the American scene). His preaching can even be considered conservative in the sense that he dared to return to the notion of good and evil, to invoke the concept of a human nature, and to believe that God in Jesus Christ is the final arbiter of history—concepts long dismissed and derided by secular minds. His faith was strong at center but had a remarkable openness in its structure. He stressed that God's "common grace" was shared by secularists as well as Christians. At the same time, he was unsparing of any form of self-satisfaction in the church, an attitude which explained in part his acceptance by many humanists, socialists, and men of other faiths. He loved the church, but he criticized it for its failure to provide moral leadership.

One final note of warning: in communicating the gospel to the secular mind, Niebuhr's particular method may not be the appropriate method for everyone. Sharing the gospel means at least two things: the essence of the gospel must be presented in such a way that it may be seen and heard for what it truly is; it must also be presented in such a way that it may be either accepted or rejected. There are numerous ways to present the good news with clarity; there are no guaranteed ways to present it so that it will be accepted. Using common human experience as a base, Niebuhr sought to show that the secular view of life is inadequate: the secular analysis of man made less sense than the biblical one. He knew that the refutation of secular presuppositions did not compel the secularist to accept the Christian faith, but it gave the gospel an opportunity to be heard.

Karl Barth had little interest in speaking the Word to the world. Paul Tillich was so alert to the nuances of the world that he may have blurred the message of the Word. Niebuhr tried to keep a healthy tension between the Word and the

world. Niebuhr's doctrine of sin has communicated to both
church and world in spite of its complications (if only he
could have spoken in parables as well as he spoke in paradoxes), but his doctrine of grace has failed to speak adequately to either. His preaching method is partly to blame
for his lack of communication about God's grace: he spoke
more often of sin, and since the life of grace is still mixed
with evil it is easier to stress man's condition of sin. Yet it is
too much to ask of any preacher that his every word be as
good as his best word. But this is a surface reason and does
not probe the deeper cause. St. Paul held that the gospel is a
scandal to the unregenerate because his whole existence is
perverted. Niebuhr labeled this perversion "Harvard orthodoxy"—to accept the Christian analysis of the human situation without accepting the Christian remedy. Secularists
will continue to stumble at any solution based on the person
and work of a historical Christ.

After reading Niebuhr again in the preparation of this
book, I am now more than ever persuaded that his thought
can be a source of critical guidance to a new generation.
His deep faith in God's transcendent judgment and mercy
can once again support and illumine thoughtful people both
inside and outside the Christian circle. He deserves to be
heard again.

Notes

CHAPTER ONE

1. Reinhold Niebuhr, "Intellectual Autobiography," in *Reinhold Niebuhr: His Religious, Social, and Political Thought,* The Library of Living Theology, vol. 2, ed. Charles Kegley and Robert W. Bretall (New York: Macmillan Co., 1956), p. 3 (hereafter cited as Niebuhr, "Intellectual Autobiography").

2. Ibid.   3. Ibid.   4. Ibid., p. 20.

5. June Bingham, *Courage to Change: An Introduction to the Life and Thought of Reinhold Niebuhr* (New York: Charles Scribner's Sons, 1961), p. 11.

6. Nathan A. Scott, Jr., *Reinhold Niebuhr* (Minneapolis: University of Minnesota Press, 1963), p. 25.

7. Ibid., p. 43.   8. Niebuhr, "Intellectual Autobiography," p. 3.

9. Bingham, p. 83.   10. Niebuhr, "Intellectual Autobiography," p. 4.   11. Ibid., p. 5.

12. Reinhold Niebuhr, *Leaves from the Notebook of a Tamed Cynic,* Living Age Books (New York: Meridian Books, 1959), p. 20 (hereafter cited as Niebuhr, *Tamed Cynic*).

13. Ibid., p. 22.   14. Ibid., p. 45.

15. Niebuhr, "Intellectual Autobiography," p. 6.

16. Ibid., p. 7.

17. Reinhold Niebuhr, "Ten Years That Shook My World," *Christian Century* 56 (April 26, 1939): 545.

18. Martin E. Marty, "Reinhold Niebuhr: Public Theology and the American Experience," *The Journal of Religion* 54 (October 1974): 344.

19. Niebuhr, "Intellectual Autobiography," p. 7.

20. Niebuhr, *Tamed Cynic*, p. 175.

21. Niebuhr, "Ten Years That Shook My World," p. 542.

22. Ibid.

23. Niebuhr, "Intellectual Autobiography," p. 6.

24. Reinhold Niebuhr, *Does Civilization Need Religion?* (New York: Macmillan Co., 1927), pp. 9–10.

25. Niebuhr, "Intellectual Autobiography," p. 7.

26. Niebuhr, *Tamed Cynic*, pp. 218–19.

27. Niebuhr, "Intellectual Autobiography," p. 8.

28. Ibid., pp. 8–9.

29. Reinhold Niebuhr, *Moral Man and Immoral Society* (New York: Charles Scribner's Sons, 1932), pp. 257, 259.

30. Ibid., p. xi.   31. Ibid., p. xxiii.   32. Ibid., p. 95.

33. Ibid., p. 107.

34. Reinhold Niebuhr, *The Contribution of Religion to Social Work* (New York: Columbia University Press, 1932), p. 49.

35. Reinhold Niebuhr, *Reflections on the End of an Era* (New York: Charles Scribner's Sons, 1934), p. ix.

36. Ibid.   37. Ibid., p. 136.   38. Ibid., pp. 284–85.

39. Reinhold Niebuhr, *An Interpretation of Christian Ethics*, Living Age Books (New York: Meridian Books, 1956), p. 38.

40. Ibid., p. 9.   41. Ibid., p. 192.   42. Ibid., p. 50.

43. Ibid., p. 55.   44. Ibid., p. 83.   45. Ibid., p. 153.

46. Reinhold Niebuhr, *Beyond Tragedy* (New York: Charles Scribner's Sons, 1937), p. x.

47. Niebuhr, "Intellectual Autobiography," p. 9.

48. Niebuhr, *Beyond Tragedy*, p. 13.

49. Quoted in Bingham, p. 23.

50. Bingham, pp. 44–45.

51. Robert McAfee Brown, "Reinhold Niebuhr: A Study in Humanity and Humility," *The Journal of Religion* 54 (October 1974): 325.

52. John C. Bennett, "The Greatness of Reinhold Niebuhr," *Union Seminary Quarterly Review* 2 (Fall 1971): 8.

53. Niebuhr, "Intellectual Autobiography," p. 9.

54. Emil Brunner, "Some Remarks on Reinhold Niebuhr's Work as a Christian Thinker," in *Reinhold Niebuhr: His Religious, Social, and Political Thought*, p. 28.

55. Reinhold Niebuhr, *Christianity and Power Politics* (New York: Charles Scribner's Sons, 1940), p. ix.

56. Ibid., pp. 1–2.   57. Ibid., p. 33.

58. Reinhold Niebuhr, *The Children of Light and the Children of Darkness* (New York: Charles Scribner's Sons, 1944), p. xiii.

59. Ibid., pp. 10–11.   60. Ibid., pp. 40–41.

61. Gabriel Fackre, *The Promise of Reinhold Niebuhr* (Philadelphia: J. B. Lippincott Company, 1970), p. 24.

62. Reinhold Niebuhr, *Discerning the Signs of the Times* (New York: Charles Scribner's Sons, 1946), p. x.

63. Niebuhr, "Intellectual Autobiography," p. 9.

64. Reinhold Niebuhr, *Faith and History* (New York: Charles Scribner's Sons, 1949), p. 164.

65. Ibid., p. viii.   66. Ibid., p. 120.   67. Ibid., p. 139.

68. Ibid., p. 150.

69. Reinhold Niebuhr, *The Irony of American History* (New York: Charles Scribner's Sons, 1952), p. viii.

70. Ibid.   71. Ibid., p. 155.   72. Ibid., p. 23.

73. Fackre, p. 26.

74. Reinhold Niebuhr, *Christian Realism and Political Problems* (New York: Charles Scribner's Sons, 1953), p. 2.

75. Reinhold Niebuhr, *The Self and the Dramas of History* (New York: Charles Scribner's Sons, 1955), p. 4.

76. Ibid.   77. Ibid., pp. 4–5.

78. Reinhold Niebuhr, *Pious and Secular America* (New York: Charles Scribner's Sons, 1958), p. 2.

79. Ibid.

80. Reinhold Niebuhr, *The Structure of Nations and Empires* (New York: Charles Scribner's Sons, 1959), p. 31.

81. Ibid., p. 267.   82. Ibid.   83. Ibid., p. 282.

84. Ibid., p. 291.

85. Reinhold Niebuhr and Alan Heimart, *A Nation So Conceived* (New York: Charles Scribner's Sons, 1963), p. 126.

86. Ibid., p. 127.   87. Ibid., p. 155.

88. Reinhold Niebuhr and Paul E. Sigmund, *The Democratic Experience* (New York: Frederick A. Praeger Publishers, 1969), p. vi.

89. Reinhold Niebuhr, *Man's Nature and His Communities* (New York: Charles Scribner's Sons, 1965), p. 23.

90. Ibid., p. 24.   91. Ibid.   92. Ibid., pp. 15–16.

93. Reinhold Niebuhr, *Justice and Mercy*, ed. Ursula M. Niebuhr (New York: Harper & Row, 1974), p. 5.

CHAPTER TWO

1. Niebuhr, *The Nature and Destiny of Man*, two volumes in one (New York: Charles Scribner's Sons, 1953), 1: 124.

2. Ibid., p. 4.   3. Ibid., p. 5.   4. Ibid., pp. 27–28.

5. Ibid., p. 75.   6. Ibid., p. 84.   7. Ibid., p. 33.

8. Ibid., p. 39.   9. Ibid., p. 40.   10. Ibid., p. 53.

11. Ibid., p. 81.   12. Ibid.   13. Ibid., p. 87.

14. Ibid., p. 92.   15. Ibid.   16. Ibid., p. 112.

17. Ibid., p. 24.

18. William John Wolf, "Reinhold Niebuhr's Doctrine of Man," in *Reinhold Niebuhr: His Religious, Social, and Political Thought*, pp. 231–32.

19. Niebuhr, *The Nature and Destiny of Man*, 1: 123–24.

20. Reinhold Niebuhr, "Reply to Interpretation and Criticism," in *Reinhold Niebuhr: His Religious, Social, and Political Thought*, p. 433 (hereafter cited as Niebuhr, "Reply").

21. Ibid., p. 439.   22. Niebuhr, *Beyond Tragedy*, pp. 5–6.

23. Niebuhr, *The Nature and Destiny of Man*, 1: 128.

24. Ibid., p. 131.   25. Ibid., pp. 140–45.   26. Ibid., p. 150.

27. Ibid., pp. 163–64.   28. Ibid., p. 166.

29. Reinhold Niebuhr, "Christian Faith and Natural Law," in *Love and Justice*, ed. D. B. Robertson (Philadelphia: Westminster Press, 1957), p. 54.

30. Niebuhr, *Discerning the Signs of the Times*, p. 65.

CHAPTER THREE

1. Daniel Day Williams, *God's Grace and Man's Hope* (New York: Harper & Bros., 1949), p. 28.

2. Niebuhr, *The Contribution of Religion to Social Work*, p. 66.

3. Niebuhr, *The Self and the Dramas of History*, p. 41.

4. Niebuhr, *Faith and History*, p. 31.

5. Niebuhr, *Christianity and Power Politics*, p. 63.

6. Niebuhr, *Pious and Secular America*, p. 126.

7. Niebuhr, *The Nature and Destiny of Man*, 1: 180.

8. Ibid.   9. Ibid., p. 181.   10. Ibid., p. 251.

11. Ibid., p. 182.   12. Ibid., p. 185.   13. Ibid., p. 252.

14. Niebuhr, *An Interpretation of Christian Ethics*, p. 81.

15. Niebuhr, *The Nature and Destiny of Man*, 1: 191.

16. Ibid., p. 199.   17. Ibid., p. 200.   18. Ibid., p. 208.

19. Ibid., p. 213.   20. Bingham, p. 141.   21. Ibid.

22. Niebuhr, *The Nature and Destiny of Man*, 1: 179.

23. Ibid., p. 232.   24. Ibid., p. 233.   25. Ibid., p. 239.

26. Ibid., p. 242.   27. Ibid., p. 251.   28. Ibid., p. 255.

29. Ibid., p. 263.

30. Niebuhr, *The Self and the Dramas of History*, p. 135.

31. Niebuhr, *The Nature and Destiny of Man*, 1: 269.

CHAPTER FOUR

1. Niebuhr, "Reply," p. 437.

2. Niebuhr, *The Nature and Destiny of Man*, 2: 108.

3. Niebuhr, *Pious and Secular America*, p. 105.

4. Reinhold Niebuhr, "Literalism, Individualism, and Billy Graham," in *Essays in Applied Christianity*, ed. D. B. Robertson, Living Age Books (New York: Meridian Books, 1959), p. 129.

5. Niebuhr, "Our Dependence is on God," in *Essays in Applied Christianity*, p. 335.

6. Niebuhr, "Reply," p. 439.

7. Paul Lehmann, "The Christology of Reinhold Niebuhr," in *Reinhold Niebuhr: His Religious, Social, and Political Thought*, p. 253.

8. Ibid., p. 264.

9. Niebuhr, *The Nature and Destiny of Man*, 1: 200.

10. Niebuhr, *The Nature and Destiny of Man*, 2: 37.

11. Ibid., p. 58.   12. Ibid., p. 77.   13. Ibid., pp. 85–89.

14. Ibid., p. 92.   15. Ibid., p. 99.   16. Ibid., pp. 108–109.

17. Ibid., pp. 110–14.   18. Ibid., p. 114.   19. Ibid., p. 127.

20. Ibid., p. 143.   21. Ibid., pp. 169–70.   22. Ibid., p. 148.

23. Ibid., p. 198.   24. Ibid., p. 153.   25. Ibid., p. 156.

26. Ibid., pp. 211–12.   27. Ibid., p. 156.   28. Ibid., p. 213.

29. Ibid., p. 288.   30. Niebuhr, *Beyond Tragedy*, p. 188.

31. Niebuhr, *The Nature and Destiny of Man*, 2: 291–92.

32. Ibid., p. 294.

CHAPTER FIVE

1. Niebuhr, *The Irony of American History*, p. 63.

2. Niebuhr, *The Nature and Destiny of Man*, 2: 190.

3. Niebuhr, *Does Civilization Need Religion?*, p. 12.

4. Reinhold Niebuhr, "Christian Faith and Social Action," in *Christian Faith and Social Action*, ed. J. A. Hutchison (New York: Charles Scribner's Sons, 1953), pp. 238–39 (hereafter cited as Niebuhr, "Christian Faith and Social Action").

5. Niebuhr, *The Nature and Destiny of Man*, 2: 248.

6. Ibid., p. 284.

7. Niebuhr, *Moral Man and Immoral Society*, p. xi.

8. Niebuhr, "Christian Faith and Social Action," p. 241.

9. Niebuhr, *Faith and History*, p. 189.

10. Niebuhr, *The Nature and Destiny of Man*, 1: 219ff.

11. Ibid., 2: 247.

12. Niebuhr, *Faith and History*, p. 226.

13. Reinhold Niebuhr, "The Ethic of Jesus and the Social Problem," in *Love and Justice*, p. 253 (hereafter cited as Niebuhr, "The Ethic of Jesus and the Social Problem").

14. Niebuhr, "Christian Faith and Social Action," p. 230.

15. Niebuhr, *Discerning the Signs of the Times*, p. 56.

16. Bennett, "Reinhold Niebuhr's Social Ethics," in *Reinhold Niebuhr: His Religious, Social, and Political Thought*, pp. 50–51.

17. Reinhold Niebuhr, "Which Question Comes First for the Church?," in *Essays in Applied Christianity*, p. 88.

18. Niebuhr, *Christianity and Power Politics*, p. 219.

19. Reinhold Niebuhr, "The Weakness of the Modern Church," in *Essays in Applied Christianity*, pp. 69–70 (hereafter cited as Niebuhr, "The Weakness of the Modern Church").

20. Reinhold Niebuhr, "We Are Men and Not God," in *Essays in Applied Christianity*, pp. 172–73.

21. Reinhold Niebuhr, "The Oxford Conference on Church and State," in *Essays in Applied Christianity*, p. 296.

22. Niebuhr, *Pious and Secular America*, pp. 20–21.

23. Niebuhr, *Faith and History*, p. 239.

24. Reinhold Niebuhr, "The Ecumenical Issue in the United States," in *Essays in Applied Christianity*, p. 275.

25. Reinhold Niebuhr, "The Idolatry of America," in *Love and Justice*, p. 97.

26. Reinhold Niebuhr, "The Weakness of the Modern Church," p. 76.

27. Niebuhr, *The Nature and Destiny of Man*, 2: 217.

28. Niebuhr, "The Ethic of Jesus and the Social Problem," p. 38.

29. Niebuhr, *Beyond Tragedy*, p. 60.

CHAPTER SIX

1. Paul Merkley, *Reinhold Niebuhr: A Political Account* (Montreal, Canada: McGill-Queen's University Press, 1975), p. viii. In this well-written book Merkley says that his entire argument is that Niebuhr's unmatched political influence is due to the theological ground of his work, and "that in Niebuhr's own intellectual pilgrimage theological commitment has been the prime mover" (p. ix).

2. Patrick Granfield, *Theologians at Work* (New York: Macmillan Co., 1967), p. 55.

3. John C. Bennett, "The Greatness of Reinhold Niebuhr," *Union Seminary Quarterly Review* 27 (Fall 1971): 4.

4. Ibid.

Selected Bibliography

PRINCIPAL WORKS OF REINHOLD NIEBUHR

Does Civilization Need Religion?—A Study in the Social Resources and Limitations of Religion in Modern Life. New York: Macmillan Co., 1927.

Leaves from the Notebook of a Tamed Cynic. Living Age Books. New York: Meridian Books, 1959.

The Contribution of Religion to Social Work. New York: Columbia University Press, 1932.

Moral Man and Immoral Society: A Study in Ethics and Politics. New York: Charles Scribner's Sons, 1932.

Reflections on the End of an Era. New York: Charles Scribner's Sons, 1934.

An Interpretation of Christian Ethics. Living Age Books. New York: Meridian Books, 1956.

Beyond Tragedy: Essays on the Christian Interpretation of History. New York: Charles Scribner's Sons, 1937.

Christianity and Power Politics. New York: Charles Scribner's Sons, 1940.

The Nature and Destiny of Man: A Christian Interpretation. Two volumes in one. Vol. 1, *Human Nature.* Vol. 2, *Human Destiny.* New York: Charles Scribner's Sons, 1953.

The Children of Light and the Children of Darkness: A Vindication of Democracy and a Critique of Its Traditional Defense. New York: Charles Scribner's Sons, 1944.

Discerning the Signs of the Times: Sermons for Today and Tomorrow. New York: Charles Scribner's Sons. 1946.

Faith and History: A Comparison of Christian and Modern Views of History. New York: Charles Scribner's Sons, 1949.

The Irony of American History. New York: Charles Scribner's Sons, 1952.

Christian Realism and Political Problems. New York: Charles Scribner's Sons, 1953.

The Self and the Dramas of History. New York: Charles Scribner's Sons, 1957.

Love and Justice. Edited by D. B. Robertson. Philadelphia: Westminster Press, 1957.

The World Crisis and American Responsibility. Edited by Ernest W. Lefever. New York: Association Press, 1958.

Pious and Secular America. New York: Charles Scribner's Sons, 1958.

Essays in Applied Christianity. Edited by D. B. Robertson. New York: World Publishing Co., Meridian Books, 1959.

The Structure of Nations and Empires: A Study of the Recurring Patterns and Problems of the Political Order in Relation to the Unique Problems of the Nuclear Age. New York: Charles Scribner's Sons, 1959.

Reinhold Niebuhr on Politics. Edited by Harry R. Davis and Robert C. Good. New York: Charles Scribner's Sons, 1960.

A Nation So Conceived: Reflections on the History of America from Its Early Vision to Its Present Power. With Alan Heimert. New York: Charles Scribner's Sons, 1963.

Man's Nature and His Communities. New York: Charles Scribner's Sons, 1965.

Faith and Politics: A Commentary on Religious, Social, and Political Thought in a Technological Age. Edited by Ronald H. Stone. New York: George Braziller, 1968.

The Democratic Experience: Past and Prospects. With Paul E. Sigmund. New York: Frederick A. Praeger Publishers, 1969.

Justice and Mercy. Edited by Ursula M. Niebuhr. New York: Harper & Row, 1974.

BOOKS ABOUT REINHOLD NIEBUHR

Bingham, June. *Courage to Change: An Introduction to the Life and Thought of Reinhold Niebuhr.* New York: Charles Scribner's Sons, 1961.

Fackre, Gabriel J. *The Promise of Reinhold Niebuhr,* The Promise of Theology series, ed. Martin E. Marty. Philadelphia: J. B. Lippincott Co., 1970.

Guthrie, Shirley Caperton, Jr. *The Theological Character of Reinhold Niebuhr's Social Ethic.* Winterthur, Switzerland: P. G. Keller Verlag, 1959.

Harland, Gordon. *The Thought of Reinhold Niebuhr.* New York: Oxford University Press, 1960.

Hofmann, Hans. *The Theology of Reinhold Niebuhr.* Translated by Louise Pettibone Smith. New York: Charles Scribner's Sons, 1956.

Kegley, Charles W., and Robert W. Bretall, eds. *Reinhold Niebuhr: His Religious, Social, and Political Thought.* The Library of Living Theology, vol. 2. New York: Macmillan Co., 1956.

Landon, Harold R., ed. *Reinhold Niebuhr: A Prophetic Voice in Our Time.* Greenwich, Conn.: Seabury Press, 1962.

Merkley, Paul. *Reinhold Niebuhr: A Political Account.* Montreal, Canada: McGill-Queen's University Press, 1975.

Scott, Nathan A., Jr., ed. *The Legacy of Reinhold Niebuhr.* Chicago: University of Chicago Press, 1975.

Stone, Ronald H. *Reinhold Niebuhr: Prophet to Politicians.* Nashville, Tenn.: Abingdon Press, 1972.

A thorough record of Niebuhr's books, essays, and periodical articles through the year 1953 is found in D. B. Robertson's *Reinhold Niebuhr's Works: A Bibliography* (Berea, Ky.: Berea College Press, 1954). Professor Robertson reissued and extended this bibliography through the year 1955 in *Reinhold Niebuhr: His Religious, Social, and Political Thought,* ed. Charles W. Kegley and Robert W. Bretall. Ronald H. Stone and Joann M. Stone have updated Robertson's work in "The Writings of Reinhold Niebuhr, 1953–1971," *Union Seminary Quarterly Review* 5, no. 27 (Fall 1971): 9–27. A complete bibliography on Niebuhr is yet to be compiled but these works come close.